"*Reversing the Senses* is the perfect combination of personal story, theory, and practical steps . . . I have applied the principles both with individuals and among the leaders in our company and we have moved farther forward in the last eighteen months than we had in the previous decade.  I highly recommend your willingness to apply these simple truths.

—BRIAN J. FLORNES,
VINTAGE SENIOR LIVING

"The principles that Hubbard discusses are timeless. What makes his work unique and effective is his ability to bring it to life and make it real for the participant. I have found that by applying these principles, I am able to positively impact my own thoughts and, accordingly, my emotions. I have also noticed a dramatic improvement with my leadership team in their ability to work together more effectively. I highly recommend Hubbard and his work."

—SEAN SMITH, CEO,
KEENAN AND ASSOCIATES

"Through Hubbard's development of the Core Process, he has allowed us as observers of and participants in the Universe to understand fully how to slow down the metabolism of the mind to successfully live in the present. *Reversing the Senses* allows us all to recognize and act upon the fact that what takes place in our lives is a result of our own inner thoughts, emotions, and outlook. Hubbard teaches us to create our existence by harnessing the positive energy force that is around us all."

—DR. PHILIP K. ANTHONY, CEO,
DECISIONQUEST

"Martin Hubbard, through his unique abilities, perspectives, and processes, has captured and shares what the obstacles and the root causes are that are limiting high achievers from experiencing ultimate fulfillment, happiness, and real success in their lives. Through personal experience and years of application and research, he has discovered the prescription for unlocking the senses and provides a simple path to achieving and maximizing one's own personal capacity to lead and achieve."

—GREG PALMER, FOUNDER,
GPALMER AND ASSOCIATES

"*Reversing the Senses* caused a paradigm shift in how I look at and feel about myself. It was a helpful tool in changing misconceived notions I felt about myself that, in turn, has made me a more genuine person and effective leader. Martin Hubbard shows how positive attitude as a foundation historically is so key to joy as it logically combines the words and concepts of many great leaders, philosophers, and teachers to illustrate life-changing techniques for a more fulfilled life. Thank you, Martin, for your phenomenal work."

—JAMES F. CHAPEL, PRESIDENT,
FINANCIAL BENEFITS GROUP, LLC

"What a thought-provoking and behavior-changing book! Doing the same thing over and over but expecting different results sure wasn't working for me. I now have the tools and different perspective to make life-changing improvements to my life. I'm not the only one to benefit. My friends and loved ones are positively affected by my health and personal growth."

—GREGG KELLY, FORMER CEO,
   ORTHODYNE ELECTRONICS

"Martin Hubbard is one of those unique individuals who can transform his life experience into meaningful and informative ideas for others to consider. His book provides the reader with a great intellectual understanding not only of how we can change our lives for the better but also of how we can take constructive action to change our experience of life. Hubbard does a wonderful job of showing the reader how the road to serenity and personal freedom can begin right now. I highly recommend taking the first step by reading his book."

—GARY CARMELL, CFA,
   PRESIDENT-PARTNER,
   CWS CAPITAL PARTNERS LLC

REVERSING

THE

SENSES

REVERSING

THE

SENSES

INCREASING YOUR INTERNAL CAPACITY
TO LEAD AND ACHIEVE

MARTIN HUBBARD

with STEPHEN PALMER

RIVER GROVE
BOOKS

Published by River Grove Books
Austin, TX
www.rivergrovebooks.com

Distributed by River Grove Books

For ordering information or special discounts for bulk purchases, please contact River Grove Books at PO Box 91869, Austin, TX 78709, 512.891.6100.

Design and composition by Greenleaf Book Group LLC
Cover design by Greenleaf Book Group LLC
Cover image: ©iStockphoto.com/Rogotanie

Cataloging-in-Publication data
Hubbard, Martin, 1960-
    Reversing the senses : increasing your internal capacity to lead and achieve / Martin Hubbard, with Stephen Palmer.—1st ed.
       p. ; cm.
    Issued also as an ebook.
    Includes bibliographical references.
    1. Success in business—Psychological aspects. 2. Businesspeople—Psychology. 3. Achievement motivation. 4. Attitude (Psychology) 5. Leadership. I. Palmer, Stephen, 1976- II. Title.
HF5386 .H83 2014
650.1   2013956791

    ISBN: 978-1-938416-56-9
    eBook ISBN: 978-1-938416-58-3

First Edition

CONTENTS

FOREWORD

I have spent the past twenty years committed to playing a pivotal role in successful technology and business development in pharmaceutical, medical device, and healthcare markets. During my tenure as president of Allergan Medical, I had the opportunity to meet Martin for the first time through our common affiliation with the Young Presidents Organization back when he was a hard-charging CEO. Over the ensuing ten years, we have become close personal friends as well as sharing common interest in the area of thought and emotional development and their impact on individual and organizational performance.

There is no more important endeavor in life than understanding and developing solid personal internal foundations. The axiom "In order to do, first you must be" not only rings true but also, if fully understood and pursued, will lead to achievement for the individual beyond his or her comprehension. The principles discussed in *Reversing the Senses*, and the simple steps of the Core Process, are the tools required to develop, improve, and enhance your foundation.

My own personal experience, whether running a Fortune 500 company or simply managing my day, has demonstrated that by developing your internal capacity you are able to handle the most difficult and challenging situations with relative ease and confidence. I am not saying there are not times that are stressful, because most definitely there are! I remember while leading my team as CEO and president of Bausch+Lomb Surgical, many pivotal decisions required much more than intellect to make. During these times, the ability of my team and me to rely on our emotional intelligence to navigate, think clearly, and perform proved to be the deciding factors to our success.

I cannot overstate the importance of being able to visualize your success in your own mind, even if your circumstances may not clearly indicate this success is within your reach. The process of reversing your senses as an exercise has proved to be invaluable to me in accomplishing this time and again. This is why I have made it a priority for my executive teams to understand these principles and develop their own practice for how they think and what they think regarding the achievement of any goal or endeavor.

In my most recent business venture, ALPHAEON, my management team and I are putting these principles to their full test as we embark on creating a disruptive business model in the Lifestyle Healthcare industry. I am confident our success, as in prior successes, is rooted in our ability to apply the principles of thought and emotional development to the fullest extent.

In order to effectively lead, you must embody the principles you espouse. Martin is an individual who not only understands these principles; he also lives them. His commitment to helping others do the same in this book is genuine. If you are interested in improving your internal capacity to lead and achieve, read and pay attention to *Reversing the Senses*. Apply the principles outlined by Martin and trust what will follow— more personal power, influence, and achievement than you ever dreamed possible. This has been my experience and I am confident it will be yours.

—ROBERT E. GRANT, CEO, ALPHAEON

INTRODUCTION

THE PARADOX OF
"HIGH ACHIEVER SYNDROME"

This book is for high achievers who still want more. You've achieved business and financial success at some level, yet you still feel a nagging sense of dissatisfaction or fear that it's not enough. You feel like something is missing. You may feel that the effort required to achieve your ultimate goals is just not sustainable.

You've been driven your whole life by external results. Now what you want more than anything is internal peace, a sense of fulfillment and confidence that you are truly on the right path to make your ultimate dreams a reality. Or perhaps you've hit "ceilings of complexity" and are struggling to break through. You know you can achieve even more, but you're not sure how to get to the next level.

It's one of life's great ironies that many high achievers are unhappy and unfulfilled. Their ambition and drive has taken them to places few ever arrive at. Because they never pause to enjoy the fruits of their labor or savor the essential moments of their lives, however, that same ambition and drive leaves them perpetually dissatisfied. Instead, they continue an unfulfilling and unending pursuit of the next big thing. For high achievers, successes cannot live up to their lofty anticipations of "true success" or satisfy their ultimate ambitions to achieve "greatness." In many situations, they are all but blind to the good in their life, focusing instead on negatives and shortcomings.

As a result, high achievers often put tremendous pressure on themselves and are even reluctant or unwilling to accept praise or recognition for their achievements. Haunted by a personal conviction that they are destined to fail, obsessing over the inadequacies in their lives and in those around them—yet driven by an overwhelming desire to achieve greatness—they have no time to truly live life. High achievers are consumed by visions of the future while, in the present, negative perceptions of the world and themselves control their thoughts and actions.

As Harold Kushner wrote in his book, *Living a Life that Matters: Resolving the Conflict Between Conscience and Success*, "Many apparently successful people feel that their success is undeserved and that one day people will unmask them for the frauds they are. For all the outward trappings of success, they feel hollow inside. They can never rest and enjoy their accomplishments. They need one new success after another. They need constant reassurance from the people around them to still the quiet voice inside that keeps saying, 'If other people knew you the way I know you, they would know what a phony you are.'"

If this sounds familiar, please understand that I don't write this to pass judgment. I write it because I've been exactly where you are. I know exactly how you feel. I've struggled with "high achiever syndrome" almost my entire life. I've been plagued by despair, loneliness, and discontentment that anyone looking at my "successful" life from the outside wouldn't suspect or understand.

I believe the knowledge in this book is what you've been thirsting for. I don't claim to be the authority on your life. I don't claim to have all the answers. I do claim this, however: I have been where you are and have had to find my own answers to the same struggles you face. I sincerely hope you find my discoveries useful in your own life.

My objectives in writing this book are twofold: First, it is to help you gain greater clarity, perspective, and understanding of the principles that produce internal harmony and lead to external success. Second, it is to motivate you to apply these principles in a meaningful way to develop your internal capacity to lead and achieve—to break through your ceilings and take your life to a whole new level.

All too often our most well-intentioned thoughts get sabotaged by negative, fear-based feelings. And, conversely, at times we can feel drawn to greatness, but negative thoughts drown out those feelings. I've created what I call the "Core Process" to help my clients "reverse their senses."

Let me explain what I mean by "reversing the senses." We are sensing beings. We explore the world through sight, touch, smell, taste, and hearing. Then, of course, we use our brains to process the things we've sensed and the experiences we've had. We try to make sense of our experiences, to draw lessons from them. Our experiences are translated into feelings, and these feelings give us clues to how we should think and act.

But what if our feelings are not based in reality? What if they are merely misinterpretations of events? Furthermore, what if those distorted feelings, based on misinterpretations, get embedded into our neurological wiring and cause us to think, feel, and react in ways that sabotage us and prevent us from reaching our goals?

For example, what if, as a child, you failed a spelling test and you felt embarrassed by it. A limiting, though understandable, misinterpretation of this event could be, "I'm a bad speller." That emotion of embarrassment gets translated into a thought-based perception, and you carry that with you throughout your life. It serves the purpose to help you avoid embarrassing situations.

That's just one simple example, but that kind of thing happens to everyone every day of our lives. We become dominated by our distorted perceptions caused by uncomfortable feelings. These misperceptions and feelings literally become hard-wired into our brains as neurological pathways. Fortunately, science is now discovering that we can change our brains through what scientists call "neuroplasticity." Neurological pathways can be changed. We can overcome limiting and destructive thought patterns from our past and form new, more empowering ones.

To reverse your senses means to challenge what you are sensing or feeling, create mental space so that you can analyze your experiences objectively, and consciously choose truthful and empowering perceptions.

It means to overcome the undertow of negative emotions and to reprogram your brain to view things differently so that you can choose and act from a positive space. It means to break free from the chains of negative emotions by acting from positive thoughts instead. In short, it means to flip the switch from feeling bad and making dumb mistakes to thinking clearly and positively and choosing wisely.

At its core, it means to realize that *feelings are not truth*. Just because a situation or an encounter with someone triggers negative emotions in you doesn't mean you're seeing the situation accurately. It doesn't mean you have to react to those emotions. It doesn't mean you have to be a slave to stimulus/response. You can choose! You can reverse the way you feel through conscious, deliberate thought processes. This does not mean you deny or repress your feelings. Rather, it allows you to change your mental dialogue regarding what your feelings mean.

By reversing the senses you can learn to recognize in any situation whether to trust your thoughts or your feelings, and to go with the right one, no matter what the other one is telling you. It is to feel one thing but to do another—to choose and act against your false instincts and in accordance with your true instincts. In short, reversing your senses is about becoming proactive instead of reactive.

By learning to reverse your senses, you will achieve internal harmony. By consistently applying the principles of the Core Process, you will develop your internal capacity to lead and achieve. While the process is simple, it is not easy. But once you begin to practice this you will find that it becomes a part of you. In the process you are literally changing yourself from the inside out.

"A life of reaction is a life of slavery, intellectually and spiritually. One must fight for a life of action, not reaction."

—RITA MAE BROWN

I've found in my own life that no amount of money or worldly acclaim can compensate for a deep and abiding sense of internal harmony—the irreplaceable feeling that comes from knowing you're on the right track, doing the right things for the right reasons, being the best you can be.

I've also discovered that all too often we "fish in the wrong ponds" in our quest to achieve more. We read business and leadership books looking for tips and strategies—things we can *do*, actions we can take. We believe we can get to the next level by revamping our business model, revolutionizing our marketing strategies, connecting with the key players, getting access to more capital, etc. The truth is that while all these things may be useful, they are not the key that unlocks new levels. They are not the true solutions to the real issues we face.

I've had a long personal journey to discover the fundamental, true source of personal growth and business and financial success.

I was born in Houston, Texas, to parents who were both high achievers—my father in academics and business, my mother in church and homemaking. I grew up in an environment that supported, rewarded, and demanded achievement. I don't know whether this demand was actually made by my parents or was simply an inference on my part. Regardless, it was the impression that was made on me and therefore the one that shaped my worldview, sense of self-worth, and attitude.

From the earliest age, I remember associating the

feelings of love and acceptance with doing something well. Whether I was behaving correctly, excelling in school, or performing athletics, I had a clear sense of being reinforced for what I perceived to be achievement in any category.

It soon became clear that the one area of my life that was crucial to constant positive reinforcement was sports. Here I surpassed my peers at a very early age, and received attention and praise for my achievements. On the court or on the field, I was clearly dominant compared to other kids my age. It was all well and good to get praise for my athletic prowess and to feel pride as a result. But I didn't realize at the time that when the drive to outshine my peers began to dominate my thoughts, I started to focus entirely on this one area. And when I began to associate love and acceptance as obtainable only through my superior athletic endeavor, I gave myself the makings of an adult disaster.

My family moved to California when I was twelve. There I continued to best other boys in sports and found even more opportunities to stand out as an athlete. But the insurmountable challenge I ultimately faced was that my genetic athletic abilities were simply not supported by my genetic physical traits. As a senior in high school, I was convinced a career as a football player must somehow be in my future. Yet with so much natural talent, there was no way to control my size (weighing in at 165 pounds and standing five-foot eight) to fit my ambition. My dreams fell short (no pun intended) and I reached a tragic conclusion: failure is completely out of our control, as based on my inability to change myself physically. Determined and headstrong nevertheless, I continued to play football throughout four years of college, with little team success. My frustration mounted.

By my senior year in college I was an internal wreck. I had just completed my final year of football as team captain with a losing record, my fiancé had just broken off our engagement, and my grades were anything but stellar. I found myself slipping into extreme escapist mode, seizing any opportunity to drink and disappear from my current reality. As this destructive behavior continued, the people close to me became concerned. Ever stubborn, I ignored their comments, certain not only that I was okay but also that I could figure out my life without their help.

Until the night when my life would change forever.

As had become my habit, I was playing a drinking game with a couple of fraternity brothers in a remote house off campus. We were about three hours into the game and fairly intoxicated when there was a frantic knock at the door. I recognized the voice behind the door as my girlfriend's, but she sounded unusually distressed. When I opened the door and she told me I needed to call home immediately, I knew something was terribly wrong. She would not tell me what.

Intoxicated and confused, I called my parents. My dad answered the phone in a tone of voice I had never heard before. He asked if it was really *me* he was talking to. Of course, I told him, who else would it be? He told me not to move and he was on his way to get me. When he told me why, I dropped to the floor and began to scream uncontrollably.

Earlier that day I had lent my car to my best friend. He was headed to his old neighborhood to meet up with some buddies, and all of them were going to circle back with us later that evening. In my condition after several hours of the drinking game, I hadn't realized they were long overdue. Apparently they were also highly intoxicated and, while speeding, missed a turn. They ran head-on into a telephone pole at 100-plus miles per hour. Everyone was killed instantly; my best friend had been driving.

My father's particular distress began when the sheriff informed my parents after the accident that their son had just been killed in an automobile accident. The confusion resulted from my friend having forgotten his wallet and my wallet sitting in the glove compartment of the car. The two of us looked similar, so the police assumed the driver was me.

The days and months that followed were a blur, filled with drunken nights that had no beginning and no end. I was in so much pain and so confused that I am still not sure how I managed to graduate from college. Once I did, I went straight into rehab.

My whole world changed when I went through treatment. I realized the root of my destructive behavior and grew to accept and understand that I didn't have to live that way anymore. It was a rebirth, and I was given a new chance at life. I could now achieve the things I knew I was destined to accomplish. Most important, I was no longer encumbered by the alcohol and other mood- and mind-altering substances that had been holding me back. I had experienced pain but had learned to heal and was determined to stop escaping. I was ready to embrace the world as a new and exciting adventure.

With this new lease on life came a new way of behaving. I became kind and optimistic in stark contrast to the deceitful and manipulating person I had been while under the influence. I learned to treat people differently, which led to more positive opportunities in my life.

Eventually, I went back to school to study psychology.

I spent the next five years both studying and working with people as an inpatient adolescent counselor until I received my master's degree in psychology. I also got married during this time and, to support my new family as well as pay for my studies, I took on two more jobs in addition to my counseling work. To be sure, I was altogether overextended. But I didn't mind for the most part because I was on the road to success. In my mind I was living the life I thought I was meant to live.

Things changed when I was unable to make enough money to cover the bills. I was always under pressure—often self-imposed—to make more money so I could live the life I thought I was supposed to want. Ambition drove me away from the counseling side of health care to the more lucrative side—growing the facility as a business.

I became involved in a venture-backed start-up company that implemented psychiatric treatment programs in hospitals. I had initially come in on the ground floor as a clinician, but quickly moved into operations to help build the organization. My desire to achieve, combined with my need for money, proved a very powerful motivation propelling me to success in this enterprise over the next four years.

By that point I was completely committed to business and creating wealth. I became interested in running my own show and, in 1994, found an opportunity to buy a business, taking a strong ownership position with a group of investors. I had no idea what a toll it would ultimately take on my life. I spent the next six years obsessed with the success of this enterprise. Initially it was exciting and invigorating. The thought of turning a distressed company into a vibrant and dynamic organization was compelling.

But as I achieved financial success and security, my marriage failed, my relationships with close friends soured, and even my health deteriorated. I could not realize it at the time, but I was slowly slipping back into the same destructive and fear-based behavior that I thought I had eradicated years earlier.

I was miserable, and it showed. But I was unaware of how my personal misery was harming both me and those I cared for most. It was another negative cycle, disguised and undecipherable, but it would have to be confronted and overcome if I were to ever experience peace in my life.

Ultimately I sold the business, creating the wealth I had so desperately desired and sacrificed so much for. But the divorce (which followed soon after the sale) created tremendous heartache in my family. I was a broken man yet again.

And, yet again, I began to seek answers. What I discovered was the process of healing and self-awareness that drives my life today.

It is easy to get distracted from the things that are important in life. Even when they seem to be so clear in our heads, it is very difficult to actualize the positive thoughts that lead to a more fulfilled life. During the divorce, my whole world was in turmoil. I was on an emotional downward spiral, reeling from years of neglecting my personal and emotional needs. Simply put, I was suffering because I could not grasp or live the truths I detail in this book.

This painful time was made worse by my inability

to think clearly and deal with the tremendous amount of hurt and emotion that shadowed every corner of my life. Most staggering of all was to realize how unhappy I had become, even though I'd been on the path to success and fulfillment. How could all my values have been so askew? How could I have simply been wrong about so much?

Financially I had momentary security, but I knew I'd eventually have to work again. I just had to find a new way to do so that wouldn't take such a toll in the future.

During this time of healing and self-realization, I began the spiritual and emotional exploration that has led me to the beliefs and understandings I hold today. These values have been forged through time and experience, through trial and error, and, most important, through honest self-appraisal, from which I learned how to reverse my senses and develop from the inside out.

It is something I could not have done on my own—and, I believe, neither can you. To reach a meaningful level of self-actualization and to determine the steps that will take our lives in the right direction, each of us needs the personal support and understanding of other high achievers—people just like you who have been similarly tested and who have ultimately embraced the truths in this book. There are those who have lived your pain. Now they live in a world of both personal peace and prosperity. These people can help guide you so that you too achieve that precious harmony.

There's a scene in the movie *Schindler's List* that has always been profoundly moving to me. Oskar Schindler, played by Liam Neeson, is on a hill overlooking the Jewish ghetto, watching as the Nazis violently and mercilessly expel the Jews. The movie is in black-and-white, but in this scene Oskar sees a little girl wearing a red coat. He watches her in fascination as she walks through the darkness, chaos, and confusion. It is in that moment that he knows exactly what he needs to do with his life. This experience was a reversal of the senses for him. Previously, although he wasn't a malicious man, he was selfish. His dominant thoughts were to capitalize on the war and make exorbitant profits from government contracts. But his feelings of altruistic compassion reversed those selfish thoughts.

The red coat symbolizes clarity. It is my sincere hope that this book will help you see your own "red coat" and experience those moments of clarity through the darkness, frustration, and confusion. Those brief moments of insight and clarity can make such a monumental and enduring difference in our lives. Clarity shows us the right path, and when we walk the right path in our lives, we experience peace and we're able to lead with greater power and achieve more than we ever thought possible. Clarity is the compass that helps us reverse our senses no matter how much we may feel pulled in an opposite direction.

Obviously, Oskar Schindler's example is extreme; your own "red coat moments" don't need to be as drastic for them to impact your life. Still, I've always appreciated the strong imagery in that scene and have found it highly applicable to my life.

A final introductory note: I want to stress that I'm not telling you what to do. I'm not the all-wise guru with all the answers. My desire is to simply present helpful information so that you can connect the dots yourself. If I can help you see the red coat, you'll know what to do. If I can show you the right pond to fish in, you'll find your own answers. More precisely, you'll discover that you've always had the answers.

And as you fish in the right pond and discover your answers, you will find that your ability to reverse your senses is honed and your internal capacity to lead and achieve is dramatically increased.

CHAPTER 1

WHAT IS "INTERNAL CAPACITY"?

"What lies behind us and what lies ahead of us are tiny matters compared to what lives within us."
—Henry David Thoreau

MICHAEL WAS AN ENERGETIC SEVEN-YEAR-OLD. LOOKing for a way to help him manage his energy, his parents enrolled him in swimming classes. Two years later, his parents divorced. While in the sixth grade, he was diagnosed with attention deficit hyperactivity disorder (ADHD). Swimming became his world, his outlet, his source of peace and confidence.

At age eleven, after achieving a record for his age group, Michael met Bob, a swimming coach who pushed him further and helped him fine-tune his technique. More age group records followed as Michael rapidly improved. Under Bob's training, he qualified for the 2000 Summer Olympics at the age of fifteen, becoming the youngest male to make a U.S. Olympic swim team in sixty-eight years. On March 30, 2001, Michael broke the world record in the 200-meter butterfly swim to become, at fifteen years and nine months, the youngest man to ever set a swimming world record.

Bob kept pushing Michael even harder. They trained for six hours a day, six days a week, without fail. During peak training, Michael swam a minimum of 80,000 meters per week—nearly fifty miles. He lifted weights three days a week. To fuel his intense routine, he consumed twelve thousand calories a day.

All that hard work paid off in the 2012 Olympics, where Michael Phelps won four gold and two silver medals, bringing his total to twenty-two Olympic medals, including eighteen gold medals (which is double the number for the second-highest record holders) and making him the most decorated Olympian of all time.

What was Michael's secret? Obviously, his hard work and dedication cannot be overstated, and without them he never would have succeeded. And his hard work over the years resulted in a remarkable physical trait: his lung capacity is a staggering *twelve liters—double the average of a typical adult male.* His unrivaled lung capacity helped him to swim longer, faster, harder, and to achieve with almost superhuman ability.

What I call your "internal capacity" can have a similar effect on your life. It can propel you to levels of success and achievement that previously have been beyond your reach. Developing your internal capacity transforms your hard work into more effective and efficient work that enables you to break through limitations. It gives you more internal peace and confidence so you make better decisions and influence people more effectively.

"Every great dream begins with a dreamer. Always remember, you have within you the strength, the patience, and the passion to reach for the stars to change the world."

—HARRIET TUBMAN

Your internal capacity is your ability to manage and leverage your inner world of thoughts and emotions and to reverse your senses when need be. It is your conscious ability to quiet your mind and create internal harmony—the peace you feel inside yourself when you have no conflict regarding who you are. A person with high internal capacity can maintain positive, optimistic, fearless, and courageous thoughts in the face of challenges and setbacks. He has the ability to understand, reason with, and control emotions. He has the instinctive ability to handle complex and difficult situations.

In short, internal capacity is your ability to think and see clearly, maintain positive and optimistic thoughts, make wise decisions, and feel calm, peaceful, and confident regardless of what is happening in your external world.

Developing your internal capacity starts when one stops asking the question, "What should I *do*?" and instead asks, "How should I *think* and *be*?" The rubber hits the road when you stop looking for answers outside yourself and begin looking for answers inside yourself.

High achievers pride themselves in their drive and work ethic—in fact, that's typically what they attribute their success to. They are constantly looking for that next breakthrough business strategy or marketing technique.

They network with other high achievers, all in an effort to figure out what they should do, what actions they should take to get to the next level. But hard work and external strategies can only take you so far.

Suppose you wanted to achieve Richard Branson's level of wealth, success, and achievement. Further suppose you were granted the opportunity to shadow him for a year. You could watch everything he did in his daily routine. You could study his business decisions. But if you were to go home and simply try to copy his actions, you would never match his success. It wouldn't be enough *to do what he does*. Ultimately, you'd have *to learn to think as he thinks, feel what he feels, and see what he sees in his internal world.* His success—like that of all ultra-achievers—has less to do with what goes on in boardrooms and more to do with what goes on between his ears. (In fact, I detail a few key components of what goes on between his ears in chapter five.)

"Our fate is shaped from within ourselves outward, never from without inward."

—JACQUES LUSSEYRAN

All ultra-achievers have incredible internal capacity, which has been forged in the fires of adversity. They have chosen to look inside themselves for answers instead of just mimicking the actions of other achievers. They are masterful decision makers because of the internal peace and clarity they experience.

Hard work, natural intelligence, and drive have taken you a long way in your life. Yet if you're like most high achievers, you still feel burdened by limitations, frustrated by complexity. Although people looking on the outside would say you're a great decision maker and confident leader, you know otherwise. You struggle with insecurities. You worry that you're not making the right decisions.

The answers you seek are not in the next book about business strategy. They are not found by copying someone else's actions. They are not found by working longer and harder. To get to the next level, you must stop working so hard and instead learn to process your thoughts and emotions more effectively. Your external results are a direct reflection of your internal capacity. The more you develop your internal capacity, the easier it will become to conquer limitations, the fewer mistakes you will make, the faster your business will grow.

Many times we don't see the ceiling until the roof starts to cave in. Such is the case for many of my clients. One in particular exemplifies this situation, and his story is worth highlighting. I started working with Jim just before the near-collapse of his business. During the couple of years prior to this point, his business had been booming. He was preparing to sell it and cash in on the years of hard work he had devoted to creating the financial security he had always dreamed of.

Unfortunately, during the process of the sale the market turned and the deal fell through. To make matters worse, he was so focused on trying to make the business look better on paper that he neglected the day-to-day management and failed to adjust for the downturn. By the time he realized he wouldn't be able to sell the business at that time, it was deep in the red and not prepared to adequately operate given the new market conditions.

When Jim got to me, his thinking was confused, he was filled with fear and anxiety, and he was uncertain how he would ultimately navigate this situation. For Jim, as for many, the focus was so much on the external that he had very little internal resources to adequately manage the complexity of his deteriorating external world. Once we're in this state it is nearly impossible to think clearly and objectively because there is so much attached to what is happening around us. Our emotions play havoc with our mind and it seems like we are going insane.

Thankfully, Jim found a happy ending by learning to shift his focus from external events to internal capacity. He was able to see how, for his entire life, he had been relying on external rewards to produce an elusive sense of happiness and satisfaction. With that realization, the flood gates opened for a new way of operating based on developing internal capacity and allowing the results to follow.

"People are like stained-glass windows. They sparkle and shine when the sun is out, but when the darkness sets in, their true beauty is revealed only if there is a light from within."

—ELISABETH KÜBLER-ROSS

The turning point for Jim came when he realized that his method of thinking, though it had gotten him far in life, was rooted in faulty beliefs. His emotions were continually reinforcing a distortion relative to sustainable success. Jim's faulty beliefs were anchored in the notion that only the strong survive and that wealth equaled strength. The story in his mind was that if you failed, you were weak. He also craved external approval and recognition because he equated them with love. This survival mentality affected everything he did in life at a subconscious level. Yes, it created his drive for success. But it did so in a way that was unhealthy and ultimately unsustainable. It created the difficult emotions that accompany the ebbs and flows of life and ultimately distorted his judgment relative to success.

The breakthrough moment of "seeing the red coat" is only the beginning. But it is critical to making any meaningful headway toward life correction, whether small or large in magnitude. Once this is achieved the real work begins. Jim experienced that moment of clarity and was then motivated to reverse his senses—to use his thoughts to overcome his destructive subconscious emotions—and to develop his internal capacity.

One of the primary techniques I guided Jim to use was mindfulness meditation, which is simply sitting quietly and learning to still your mind, become the observer of your thoughts and emotions, and gain greater awareness of your motivations and fears. I discuss the process and benefits of meditation in greater detail in chapter four.

I also helped Jim become aware of how his emotions would distort his thoughts. His most compelling emotion was anger, which came from his deeply rooted subconscious beliefs. When he felt threatened, he would get angry, and his thoughts would turn to being critical of others and wanting to control or degrade them to win and survive. With his newfound awareness, he realized he no longer needed to be held captive by anger, fear, worry, or other negative emotions.

Furthermore, Jim learned how to leverage the power of autosuggestion, through the repetition of positive mantras and belief statements, to rewrite the internal scripts that were holding him back. When he caught himself in negative self-talk, he would repeat in his mind the mantra "I am whole, strong, clear, and powerful. I am compassionate, loving, and harmonious." I detail how you can use autosuggestion in chapter six.

Through this process, he was not only able to save his business but also to direct his energy to more satisfying pursuits, both personally and professionally.

You, too, can develop your internal capacity as Jim did, by embracing, applying, and practicing the five principles of the Core Process.

CHAPTER 2

CORE PROCESS PRINCIPLE #1

YOUR THOUGHTS DETERMINE YOUR ULTIMATE RESULTS

"The thought manifests as the word, the word manifests as the deed, the deed develops into habit, and habit hardens in character . . . As we think, so we become."
—*Buddha*

IF YOU HAD TOLD ME "YOUR THOUGHTS DETERMINE your ultimate results" when I was in college, I would have said you were crazy. I would have retorted that my actions create my results, that it doesn't matter what I *think*, only what I *do*.

It wasn't until I went through rehab that I started to connect the dots—namely, my internal fears and insecurities were resulting in my drinking habit. How

I was inside was determining how I acted, which in turn dictated my results in the outside world. Presented with positive information during rehab, I learned to change my way of thinking to take a positive path in life in direct opposition to the negative one I had been on. The new insight and correction in my way of thinking was profound and struck at the core of my very being—even if I would need to understand this lesson at a deeper level later on. As a result of learning to change my thoughts, I was also able to change my actions. As my actions began to change, the world around me opened up and a new realm of possibilities presented themselves. I developed a more positive outlook and in turn made better decisions.

Simply put, our lives are shaped by our minds. What we think deep inside, where no one is looking, is who we are and who we will continue to be unless we learn to alter these thoughts. And who we are dictates what we can achieve, and how successful we can become.

> *"He who cannot change the very fabric of his thought will never be able to change reality, and will never, therefore, make any progress."*
>
> —ANWAR SADAT

This simple truth is certainly not a revelation made to me alone. It has been discussed for centuries. Leaders of major religions and philosophical schools have returned to this idea time and time again in their teachings.

What we think, how we think, and what we choose to nurture in our minds—and subsequently in our hearts—define who we are at a fundamental level. As such, you are the maker of your own fate. The life you lead is dictated by the thoughts you choose to encourage. I do not mean passing thoughts; I mean the kind of thoughts that penetrate the core of your being and shape your character. The thoughts that dictate what you love, hate, cherish, and admire. The thoughts that shape your unique perception of the world. The thoughts you nurture and justify.

Internal Thought	External Results	New Belief Mantra to Replace the Old Thought
"If I don't succeed at football, I'm a nobody."	Obsession with football, drinking to stifle the feelings of inadequacy.	I am worthwhile, important, and valuable regardless of my success in football.
"Without wealth I am weak. My money makes me strong and gives me power."	Fear and stress surrounding finances, conspicuous consumption to "prove" your wealth to the world.	I am strong and powerful. Money is simply a tool.
"I don't deserve my success. I got lucky."	Insecurity, depression, taking wrong actions to "fit in" with other people who you perceive as successful.	I am worthy of success.
"If I share my feelings, people will take advantage of me."	Not trusting, being paranoid and controlling.	Sharing my vulnerabilities makes me strong, and empowers those around me.

Internal Thought	External Results	New Belief Mantra to Replace the Old Thought
"If I say no to my childrens' requests for financial support, they will not love me."	Keeping children dependent while resenting their dependency.	Helping my children become financially self-reliant builds confidence, trust, and love in our relationship.
"I'm not a good decision maker."	Fear and hesitation, making the wrong decisions.	I am a great decision maker.
"To become financially successful, I have to take advantage of others."	Being manipulative and controlling, resulting in a bad reputation.	To become financially successful, I must create value for others.

Our harvest at the end of our lives is a direct result of the seeds—the thoughts and subsequent actions—that we have sown throughout our lives.

William James, the first educator to offer a psychology course in the United States, which occurred in the late 1800s, was likewise one of the first pioneers to teach the power of thought. As he put it, "The greatest discovery of my generation is that a human being can alter his life by altering his attitudes of mind."

James Allen, a contemporary scholar of William James, best articulated this truth in his book *As a Man Thinketh*. He explained, "You are today where your thoughts have brought you; you will be tomorrow where your thoughts take you."

Ralph Waldo Emerson, founder in the early 1800s of the Transcendentalist movement, added, "Great men are those who see that thoughts rule the world."

Then Charles F. Haanel, a successful businessman and contributor to the "New Thought Movement," came along and confirmed in his 1912 book, *The Master Key System*, "Conditions, environment, and all experiences in life are the result of our habitual, or predominant, mental attitude . . . Therefore, the secret of all power, all achievement, and all possession depends upon our method of thinking."

Napoleon Hill, one of the earliest authors in the personal success genre, who later built on the shoulders of these first pioneers, taught in his book *Think and Grow Rich* (published in 1937) that "Our brains become magnetized with the dominating thoughts which we hold in our minds, and by means with which no man is familiar, these 'magnets' attract to us the forces, the people, the circumstances of life which harmonize with the nature of our dominating thoughts."

Norman Vincent Peale published *The Power of Positive Thinking* in 1952, explaining that he developed the notion of positive thinking as a child. He says he had "the worst inferiority complex of all" and began to develop a method of positive thinking and positive philosophy in order to help himself. He then came to accept this truth, which he elegantly encapsulated as, "Change your thoughts and you change your world."

Albert Einstein, the consummate scientist, agreed with them all when he said, "The world we have created is a product of our thinking; it cannot be changed without changing our thinking."

I understand that we've been deluged in our culture with pop psychology trends and slogans that focus on positive thinking. Consequently, it can be difficult for action-oriented, results-driven, bottom-line high achievers to cut through the new age, touchy-feely fluff to see the very real and tangible effects of our thoughts. But please remember, my job is certainly not to convince you of these truths; it is simply to present information that has been profoundly useful in my life.

Fortunately, today we have access to scientific research and hard data supporting this truth, which thought pioneers and philosophers like the men quoted above never had access to. We now know scientifically that our thoughts have a profound impact on both our actions and our feelings, and obviously our life results.

Maxwell Maltz was a cosmetic surgeon who died in 1975. He was fascinated that some people, even after noticeable improvements to their appearance as the result of cosmetic surgery, still retained the same feelings of inadequacy that had prompted the surgery. His experience in his field "confirmed the fact that the 'self-image,' the individual's mental and spiritual concept or 'picture' of himself, was the real key to personality and behavior," as he wrote in his classic self-help book *Psycho-Cybernetics*. In other words, what people thought of themselves was more powerful than their physical reality. Maltz concluded, "Change the self-image and you change the personality and the behavior . . . The 'self-image' sets the boundaries of individual accomplishment. It defines what you can and cannot do. Expand the self-image and you expand the 'area of the possible.' The development of an adequate, realistic self-image will seem to imbue the individual with new capabilities, new talents and literally turn failure into success."

As Dr. Maltz researched this concept, he unearthed more and more evidence of the power of thought. As he discovered, "Experimental and clinical psychologists have proved beyond a shadow of a doubt that the human nervous system cannot tell the difference between an 'actual' experience and an experience imaged vividly in detail."

He then detailed the results of one study published in *Research Quarterly* on the effects of mental practice on improving skill in sinking basketball free throws. Three groups of basketball players were tested on their free throw performance the first and last days of the study. The first group actually practiced free throws twenty minutes every day for twenty days. The second group engaged in no practice. The third group did not practice; instead, they spent twenty minutes a day visualizing successful free throws.

The first group, those who shot free throws, improved by 24 percent. The second group, those who did nothing, showed no improvement. The third group, those who simply visualized, improved their shooting percentage by a remarkable 23 percent.

It's fascinating to me that people can improve their performance through nothing but visualization. I've experienced the power of visualization in my own practice.

For example, I've coached my clients to become better at networking and sales calls. When they're worried about important meetings, I coach them to visualize the meeting going well, from beginning to end. I tell them to see the people in the room smiling, engaged, and interested. All of my clients who practice this visualization report that their meetings go much better than expected.

In another case, one of my clients was feeling emotionally stressed from his environment. I taught him to counteract that stress whenever he felt it by visualizing the most perfect place in the world. After a week of consistent visualization he reported feeling much less stress.

Another client struggled with his seeming inability to feel empathy for others. He visualized a heart, and after a month he noticed a significant difference in his ability to feel empathy and to express his emotions.

Yet another client struggled with self-criticism and negative thoughts because of how her parents treated her as a child. She began visualizing her parents in a different light: she saw them as doing the best they could with what they were given by their parents. Over time, and as her visualizations became more clear, forgiveness came. Her ultimate visualization was of generations of a family on a picnic, talking and laughing about all the terrible things that had happened to them as children and how they had overcome them. She saw love, forgiveness, and compassion in their faces despite anything they had suffered. Her visualization exercises had a profound effect on how she felt and how she interacted with others. She became more loving, forgiving, compassionate, and peaceful. She saw herself in a better light and thus exuded more confidence.

In 1985, researchers Michael Scheier and Charles Carver published a study entitled "Optimism, Coping, and Health: Assessment and Implications of Generalized Outcome Expectancies" in *Health Psychology*. This breakthrough work, which gave scientists a method for seriously studying the healing powers of positive thinking, has now been cited in at least 3,145 other published works.

In an interview in *The Atlantic* magazine, Scheier said, "It's now safe to say that optimism is clearly associated with better psychological health, as seen through lower levels of depressed mood, anxiety, and general distress, when facing difficult life circumstances, including situations involving recovery from illness and disease."

Most researchers agree, he said, that there is a strong correlation between optimism and physical health. For example, studies are now showing that optimists are less likely to be re-hospitalized after surgery, and have decreased risk of developing heart disease and other ailments.

Scheier also reported that researchers now understand *why* optimists live happier lives than pessimists do. Optimists are not just naïve "Pollyannas," he said, but rather practical problem solvers who seek solutions to improve situations. And if they can't change situations, they're more likely to accept the reality and move on. They have better health habits than do pessimists: they're less likely to smoke, drink, or eat poorly, and they're more likely to exercise, get adequate sleep, and eat a healthy diet. Pessimists tend to deny and distort their problems and to dwell on negative feelings.

"More gold has been mined from the thoughts of men than has ever been taken from the earth."

—NAPOLEON HILL

In a study published in the *Journal of Personality and Social Psychology* in 2003, Dr. Robert Emmons, professor of psychology at the University of California, Davis, and University of Miami psychologist Michael

McCullough showed that counting blessings can actually make people feel better. In other words, our thoughts influence our emotions.

The researchers randomly divided more than one hundred undergraduates into three groups. For ten consecutive weeks, group one was asked to list five things they were grateful for from the previous week. The second group listed five things that annoyed them each week. A third group simply listed five events that had occurred each week over the course of the ten weeks.

The first group listed blessings such as these:

- Sunset through the clouds
- The chance to be alive
- The generosity of friends

The second group listed hassles such as these:

- Taxes
- Hard to find parking
- Burned my macaroni and cheese

Those who listed blessings each week had fewer health complaints, exercised more regularly, and felt better about their lives in general than either of the other two groups did.

I use gratitude on a daily basis to reverse my own senses. I have a gratitude list that I keep in my mind. Whenever I begin to feel discontentment with events in my life, I simply observe my negative thoughts and begin to recite my gratitude list in my mind. I do not wish for more gratitude; I simply state the things I am already grateful for. In all cases, I speak in the present tense: "I am grateful for my heath, wealth, love, and wisdom." I have found that I do not need to be specific in this practice . . . in fact, the more specific I get, the harder it is to maintain the mantra. The reversing of the senses happens because in that moment my feelings are usually not consistent with what I am repeating in my mind.

In her book *The How of Happiness: A New Approach to Getting the Life You Want*, Sonja Lyubomirsky, professor in the Department of Psychology at the University of California, Riverside, refers to gratitude as "a kind of meta-strategy for achieving happiness." "Gratitude," she says, "is wonder; it is appreciation; it is looking on the bright side of a setback; it is fathoming abundance; it is thanking someone in your life; it is thanking God; it is 'counting blessings.' It is savoring; it is not taking things for granted; it is coping; it is present-oriented."

Lyubomirsky's research demonstrates that expressing gratitude has several benefits. People who are grateful are likely to be happier, hopeful, and energetic, and they possess positive emotions more frequently. Individuals also tend to be more spiritual or religious, forgiving, empathetic, and helpful, while at the same time being less depressed, envious, or neurotic.

One of my clients, Betty, who I discuss later, is a perfect example of how developing a gratitude list and using that list on a daily basis can transform your attitude and ultimately your circumstances. Betty was extremely pessimistic, and her thoughts were filled with glass-half-empty scenarios. I coached her to develop a gratitude list, which was short and simple, but for her very powerful: "I am grateful for my life, my friends, and my health." After only one week of this practice, she reported a significant improvement in her mood and outlook on her circumstances.

"Nurture your mind with great thoughts, for you will never go any higher than you think."

—BENJAMIN DISRAELI

Still more affirmation of the power of thought comes from Martin Seligman, former president of the American Psychological Association and the man considered to be the father of "positive psychology," a relatively recent movement rooted in scientific research. In his books *Learned Optimism* and *Authentic Happiness*, Seligman differentiates between three types of happiness:

1. The "Pleasant Life": This state of happiness is about doing everything you can to amplify positive emotion. In other words, it's about feeling good.

2. The "Engaged Life": In this state of happiness, you identify your strengths and talents and use them in your work and daily life.

3. The "Meaningful Life": This highest state of happiness is about using your talents to serve others or a cause bigger than yourself.

Seligman also differentiates between optimists and pessimists. "The defining characteristic of pessimists," he says, "is that they tend to believe bad events will last a long time, will undermine everything they do, and are their own fault." Optimists, on the other hand, even when confronted with the same difficulties, take the opposite perspective about their misfortunes. To optimists, defeat is just a temporary setback. They don't take defeat personally and are unfazed by it. They view their failures and setbacks as challenges and use them as motivation to try even harder.

The good news, Seligman teaches, is that pessimism is not inescapable: people who naturally tend toward pessimism can learn to be optimists by "learning a new set of cognitive skills," which he says have been rigorously validated by leading psychologists and psychiatrists.

Seligman concludes from decades of research that "pessimists are up to eight times more likely to become depressed when bad events happen; they do worse at school, sports, and most jobs than their talents augur; they have worse physical health and shorter lives; and they have rockier interpersonal relations."

As you can see, the power of our thoughts is no longer the realm of new age pop psychology. Modern research has given us the tools and data to see how our thoughts influence every aspect of our lives. Our thoughts and actions must be in harmony with our desires in order to attain our desires. Thinking negatively renders negative outcomes, while thinking positively and productively results in positive experiences.

"All external changes in the forms of life, not having a change of consciousness at their base, do not improve the condition of the people, but generally make it worse . . . A better life can only come when the consciousness of men is altered for the better; and therefore all the efforts of those who wish to improve life should be directed to changing their own and other people's consciousness."

—LEO TOLSTOY

Managing our thoughts, therefore, becomes imperative to living a harmonious and successful life. I'll give you specific and detailed techniques for doing so in chapters four and seven.

For now, I invite you to consider a powerful analogy given by religious leader Boyd K. Packer. He explains that as a ten-year-old boy, he was put in charge of irrigating his family's fruit tree orchard. After being plowed in the spring, the irrigation ditches would fill with weeds.

One day, as he was performing his duties, the water flooded in every direction because of the weeds choking the ditch. He raced through the puddles trying to build up the bank to keep the water moving down its appointed path. But as soon as he had repaired one breach, another would pop up.

A neighbor came through the orchard and watched Boyd's frantic efforts. Then, acting from experience, he used a shovel to clear the bottom of the ditch to allow the water to flow unimpeded.

The wise neighbor told him, "If you want the water to stay in its course, you'll have to make a place for it to go."

Boyd learned a lot more than irrigation that day. Thoughts, like water, he learned, "will stay on course if we make a place for them to go. Otherwise our thoughts follow the course of least resistance, always seeking the lower levels."

(Note that in this context, he's referring to virtuous thoughts. But this also applies to fear- and worry-based thoughts as well. Without a channel, our thoughts tend to be unproductive, limiting, even harmful.)

"The mind is like a stage," he teaches. Our constant thoughts are like an act being performed on the stage. Even without conscious intention, negative or unworthy thoughts can "creep in from the wings" and try to attract our attention. "If you yield to them," Mr. Packer says, "they will enact for you on the stage of your mind anything to the limits of your toleration. They may enact a theme of bitterness, jealousy, or hatred. It may be vulgar, immoral, even depraved. When they have the stage, if you let them, they will devise the most clever persuasions to hold your attention."

He concludes that, "If you can control your thoughts, you can overcome habits, even degrading personal habits. If you can learn to master them you will have a happy life." Mr. Packer goes on to explain how to use uplifting music to put the right players on the stage of your mind.

The point is this: We constantly hear advice on controlling our thoughts. But the truth is that most of our thoughts come unbidden, and there's really not much we can do about that. What we can do, however, is choose which thoughts we give attention to, which ones we feed, and which ones we starve. We can give productive thoughts a channel while shutting down unproductive ones. The thoughts we entertain and focus on grow.

This is why consistent personal reflection is so critical. By this I mean taking a few minutes each day to just sit and ponder. Go to a quiet, secluded place where you won't be interrupted, whether it be your office, a park, or your backyard. Turn off your cell phone and get rid of any distractions. As you ponder, you become the observer of your thoughts. You become in tune with your deeper self that has the power to choose which thoughts you feed. You become more aware of your deeper motivations driving your decisions. You create space to think positive, motivational thoughts.

One of my clients, Jack, was seventy-five years old, a retired venture capitalist who was supposed to be living the good life. He had worked hard his whole life and had very few regrets because he liked what he did and how he lived.

He was a "deal guy" in the truest sense of the word. He loved the chase of a deal, the complexity and nature of the deal business, and the focus and sense of purpose it provided. He had grown accustomed to the feast or famine nature of the business and would proudly tell you he hadn't had a steady paycheck for more than forty years.

When he completed his last deal, he had amassed what to most people would be a small fortune. However, as we all know, our perceptions of how much is enough are all very relative.

Jack was not a frugal guy. He spent money like there was no tomorrow on himself and others. In his mind he would always be able to make it up on the next deal. But in retirement that principle no longer applied. There were no more deals to make. He was now living on a fixed, although quite large, income. He was not prepared for the difficulty in this new way of living and thinking.

It was a sobering moment for Jack when he realized that he would no longer be able to support his daughter and her family the way he had in the past, nor could he afford the multiple homes he owned or support his favorite charities at the same level he had in the past, while also living off his income from his principal until age ninety-five. This may seem like a problem with simple answers, but for Jack it was debilitating. In his mind, cutting back in those areas would mean he was a failure.

When Jack got to me, he was convinced that I could help him develop a strategy that would allow him to make the numbers work. What he found was a new way of thinking and dealing with his emotions that allowed him to make the necessary changes to live his life comfortably within his means.

Changing your thoughts is not easy, just as is working out when you've spent most of your life being relatively sedentary. The important thing is to take small steps in that direction. For Jack, that small step entailed one simple suggestion to himself: "I am not my feelings; I can choose to think differently than the way I feel." This allowed him to entertain the thoughts that eventually led to having the conversation with his daughter that he so feared.

Jack was worried about his daughter's reaction to his decision that he could no longer support her. Interestingly, she reacted much differently than he had expected. He was convinced she would be angry and would no longer love and respect him. What he got was the exact opposite. Once he was able to change his own thoughts regarding having the conversation, and how to have the conversation, the experience supported those new thoughts.

This was the breakthrough that propelled him to take actions in all other areas of his life not with dread, but with excitement and confidence. Jack was able to gracefully disengage from the nonprofits he felt tied to financially, and he began selling and repositioning assets to better meet his current needs. When he reversed his senses by thinking empowering thoughts, his emotions followed suit; the more productively he thought, the better he felt. Ultimately, this process led to him making decisions not based on fear but because they were the right decisions for his life and produced feelings of joy and satisfaction.

Embracing and actualizing the truth that our thoughts can alter our experience requires discipline. Since many struggle with this, it may be best achieved through outside assistance. With such encouragement and discipline, you can—as a high achiever driven to achieve but never taking the time to examine your true motivators—face the future with confidence.

Case Study: Steve Jobs

Clearly one of the most influential men of our time, Steve Jobs was a big believer in meditation to still the mind, access intuition, become more creative, stay focused, and make wiser decisions. (As you know, I'm also a big believer in the power of meditation, which I detail in chapter four.)

Jobs was a Zen Buddhist for many years. In 1974 he traveled to India in search of a spiritual guru. When he returned, he found one in his hometown of Los Altos, California: Kobun Chino Otogawa, a Japanese-born Zen master. Jobs studied at Kobun's Zen Center and they developed a close relationship, discussing life and Buddhism during midnight walks. Jobs told biographer Walter Isaacson, "I ended up spending as much time with him as I could. Zen has been a deep influence in my life ever since."

Kobun focused his teaching on developing a Zen meditation practice. He taught Jobs that "The real purpose of [practicing meditation] is to discover the wisdom which you have always been keeping with you . . . To discover yourself is to discover wisdom; without discovering yourself you can never communicate with anybody."

Jobs reported that Zen meditation taught him to concentrate and ignore distractions, as well as to trust intuition and curiosity—what Buddhists call "beginner's mind"—overanalysis and preconceptions. His

focus, which came from Zen meditation, and prefer-
ence for simplicity, which came from Zen aesthetics,
showed in Apple's products. Len Kaye, a Zen abbot
who teaches meditation to workers at Silicon Valley
companies, reported that Jobs was delighted when Kaye
began offering meditation classes to Apple employees.
Kaye said Jobs particularly wanted Apple's engineers to
learn meditation to boost their creativity.

In 1998 Jobs told *Businessweek*, "That's been one of
my mantras: focus and simplicity. Simple can be harder
than complex: You have to work hard to get your thinking clean to make it simple. But it's worth it in the end
because once you get there, you can move mountains…
It comes from saying no to 1,000 things to make sure
we don't get on the wrong track or try to do too much.
We're always thinking about new markets we could
enter, but it's only by saying no that you can concentrate on the things that are really important."

By reading between the lines, it seems clear that by
quieting his mind Jobs was able to make better business decisions.

"If you just sit and observe," Jobs said, "you will see
how restless your mind is. If you try to calm it, it only
makes it worse, but over time it does calm, and when
it does, there's room to hear more subtle things—that's

when your intuition starts to blossom and you start to see things more clearly and be in the present more. Your mind just slows down, and you see a tremendous expanse in the moment. You see so much more than you could see before. It's a discipline; you have to practice it."

Of course, I'm not suggesting that you should become a Zen Buddhist. What I am suggesting, though, is that if meditation was a powerful force behind Jobs' leadership, it can be helpful for you as well. Meditation may seem strange to those who haven't experienced its benefits, yet it clearly had a profound, tangible, and profitable impact on one of the most successful businessmen and businesses in history.

*   *   *

Stephen R. Covey, the renowned businessman and leadership guru, said, "Sow a thought, reap an action; sow an action, reap a habit; sow a habit, reap a character; sow a character, reap a destiny."

Thoughts are the foundation and beginning point of all success—or failure. Understanding this is profoundly empowering. Now you know the true source of all the dissatisfaction you feel in your life. You also know where to go to improve your life and your internal feelings.

CHAPTER 3

CORE PROCESS PRINCIPLE #2

YOUR EMOTIONS INFLUENCE YOUR THOUGHTS, AND VICE VERSA

"Your life is the sum of all the choices you make, both consciously and unconsciously. If you can control the process of choosing, you can take control of all aspects of your life. You can find the freedom that comes from being in charge of yourself."
—*Robert F. Bennett*

AFTER DETAILING THE POWER OF OUR THOUGHTS, I must point out to you that our most conscious efforts to elevate our thoughts can easily be sabotaged by our emotions. These are often harbored by our subconscious brain, which makes it extremely difficult for us to recognize when we are being influenced by them, or to even understand them and where they're coming from.

As I stated earlier, internal harmony is critical to managing your life effectively. Unfortunately, for most people this is easy to talk about in theory but very difficult to create and experience when their external world appears to be turning upside down. For my client Jim, such was the case. He experienced firsthand how his emotions completely overrode his sense of internal harmony. The influence on his thoughts at one point was so great that he was convinced he was going to lose his business and his family and live out his life alone.

But as I taught him the process of reversing his senses, he learned to overcome extreme anxiety and dread by reciting over and over again, "I am strong, I am clear, I am whole, and I am healthy. I am not my emotions and I can choose my thoughts." As he practiced this process, he began to feel less anxious and more hopeful. This led to him making better decisions and, finally, to a place where his external world began to reflect his new internal state. His mantra may appear to be simple, but his practice of repeating it was extremely powerful.

I've discussed the power of our thoughts. But understanding and managing our thoughts is just one piece of the puzzle. There is a direct connection between our thoughts and emotions. Our emotions influence our thoughts, and vice versa. To truly achieve internal harmony, we must understand and manage both. And in order to do this we must engage in the practice of reversing our senses.

It starts by understanding the right and left hemispheres of the brain. Stick with me here. The following science may seem boring, but it holds the keys that can liberate your thoughts and emotions and propel you to new levels of success.

The left hemisphere is your scientific, logical, reasonable, rational, objective, linear-thinking brain. It has no imagination: it is a calculator that considers nothing but cold, hard facts.

Within the left brain we also find Wernicke's area, just behind your left ear, and Broca's area, just forward of that, which together give you all language functions—the singular human ability to attach complex meanings to sounds. The job of Wernicke's area is to attach mental images to nouns. Broca's area's function is to translate verbs into actions on what cognitive neuroscientists call the "visuospatial sketchpad"—essentially the projection screen of imagination. Broca also coordinates the diaphragm, larynx, lips, and tongue to create vocal phonemes; in other words, the sounds made as we speak.

Whereas the left hemisphere of your brain is linguistic, the right hemisphere—also known as your subconscious mind—is visual. It has no language functions. It doesn't think conceptually in words; it perceives in visual images and uses imagination to envision possibilities. It doesn't add up one fact at a time to draw logical conclusions. It sees the whole picture, senses all data, recognizes patterns, and connects dots to give you intuitions—those gut feelings that tell you there's more than meets the eye.

Your right brain is a magical, fantastical world of art, imagination, and story where anything is possible. It does not know right from wrong, truth from fiction, nor does it care. Your right brain never sleeps; it manifests as dreams full of symbolic imagery.

Your right brain is also primarily responsible for your emotions. This presents a challenge, since the right, subconscious side of your brain can't communicate with the left side of your brain in language. It can't tell you, "Hey, you're struggling right now because deep-seated emotions from your childhood are holding you back," and go on to detail the story that caused those emotions.

"Not everything we are capable of knowing and doing is accessible to, or expressible in, language. This means that some of our personal knowledge is off limits even to our own inner thoughts! Perhaps this is why humans are so often at odds with themselves, because there is more going on in our minds than we can ever consciously know."

—RICHARD CYTOWIC

In his book *The Right Brain and the Unconscious: Discovering the Stranger Within*, neuropsychologist Dr. R. Joseph reveals,

> The right cerebral hemisphere is concerned predominantly with social and emotional perception and expression, including the storage of emotional memories.
>
> It is the initial depository of all our childhood experiences, including our feelings and impressions. Because the ability of very young children to understand and reason is limited, and as their language abilities are also not well developed, most of these very early experiences are stored only within the right brain or in a code not accessible to language.

Therefore, both the Child and Parent Egos are the result of visual and emotional images, associations, and impressions stamped into the unconscious mental system maintained by the right cerebral hemisphere. The left brain may have little knowledge or understanding as to their presence, except in regard to positive memories which may be more accessible.

The right brain having successfully experienced and stored in memory the matrix of emotions and feelings which make up the Child and Parent, can at a later time in response to certain situations act on those memories.

It can also reactivate the unconscious Child or Parent and all its attendant feelings and attitudes, much to the surprise, perplexity, or chagrin of the left half of the brain, which can only respond, "I don't know why I acted that way . . ."

The language-dependent, conscious left half of the brain cannot always gain access to the memories stored in the right half of the brain, particularly if they are negative.

Simply put, if we were hurt as a child, that memory is stored as a painful emotion in our right brain. Emotional defense mechanisms can be triggered by stimuli reminiscent of the original wound.

As children, we are good observers but poor inter-preters; we haven't yet developed the linguistic capacity to fully understand events and experiences. So we pro-cess experiences at an emotional, subconscious level, and those experiences are stored subconsciously before we have the ability to deal with them consciously. Then, as adults, we continue to be influenced in our decision making by these stored emotions—usually without our conscious awareness.

For example, I know some high achievers who were told as children, both verbally and otherwise, that they would never amount to much in life. That childhood wound has driven them to prove the critics wrong. While that drive may take them to a certain level, eventually it fizzles out because at some point they realize that nothing they do will ever be enough. No matter how much they achieve, they still feel like they're not good enough. At some point, for them to break through ceilings, they must process those emo-tions and understand their true motivations. Once they become consciously aware of those subconscious emotions, they're able to find internal peace and har-mony, fine-tune their motivations, and perform at even higher levels.

If all this sounds too much like "therapy" to you, let's get more practical here. Even if you're uncomfortable with the whole "wounded as a child" concept, it's clear that our emotions have a direct impact on our thoughts. Frustration and stress make it difficult to focus on our vision. Feeling jealous about someone else's success makes it difficult to think positive thoughts about him or her. We get cut off while driving and immediately our blood boils, our heart starts to pound, we want to hurt the jerk. Such a simple thing can seriously throw off our entire day.

Ronald Potter-Efron, anger management expert and author of *Healing the Angry Brain*, explains that when we get angry, our limbic system gets activated and our body switches into "fight or flight" mode by increasing our heart rate, respiration, and blood flow to muscles. Here's the kicker—usually this all happens without our conscious awareness, meaning it inhibits our thought processes.

Scientists from the University of Valencia recently completed a study on the brain's cardiovascular, hormonal, and asymmetric activation response when we get angry. The results, published in the journal *Hormones and Behavior*, reveal that anger provokes profound changes in the state of mind of the subjects ("they felt angered and had a more negative state of mind") and in different psychobiological parameters. When we get angry, the researchers concluded, our heart rate, arterial tension, and testosterone production increases; cortisol (the stress hormone) decreases; and the left hemisphere of the brain becomes more stimulated. Neus Herrero, main author of the study and researcher, explains: "Inducing emotions generates profound changes in the autonomous nervous system, which controls the cardiovascular response, and also in the endocrine system. In addition, changes in cerebral activity also occur, especially in the frontal and temporal lobes." (Interested readers will find more details about the study online at http://www.sciencedaily .com/releases/2010/05/100531082603.htm.)

"Individuals in unconscious disagreement with themselves can never reach full understanding with others."

—ROBERT GRUDIN

Again, the point is that it's not enough to manage our thoughts; our emotions must be monitored and managed as well. And how do we manage our emotions? Why, by our thoughts, of course! This is the essence of reversing our senses—overcoming powerful negative emotions harbored by our subconscious mind.

Dr. David D. Burns, an adjunct clinical professor of psychiatry at the Stanford University School of Medicine, is widely accepted as the expert on depression. His book, *Feeling Good*, has sold more than 4 million copies and is the book American and Canadian mental health professionals recommend most often for individuals suffering from depression. His take is that most cases of depression are not "endogenous," meaning originating as malfunction within the body. Rather, he diagnoses most cases as "reactive depression" that originates as "malfunctions" in thinking. As a cognitive therapist, he is guided by three principles:

1. All our emotions are generated by our thoughts. How we feel at any given moment is governed by what we are thinking about.
2. Depression is the constant thinking of negative thoughts.

3. Most negative thoughts that cause us emotional turmoil are usually plain wrong or at least distortions of the truth, but we accept them without question.

Dr. Burns concludes that the primary source of depression is prolonged immersion in distorted thinking. Of course, negative, self-critical thinking is one category of "distorted" thinking.

Negative thinking can create a self-reinforcing loop: We focus on negative thoughts, which puts us in a bad mood. Our emotions then make our thinking even worse. Likewise, positive thinking can create a self-reinforcing loop: Positive thoughts make us feel happy, and we continue thinking positively, just as we learned from the gratitude research I referenced in chapter two.

My ultimate goal here is to simply help you become aware of the relationship between thoughts and emotions and on the influence both have on your ultimate success. This knowledge helps us to live a more conscious life, that is, to consciously and proactively choose how we respond to events and circumstances, rather than being a reactive puppet on the strings of negative and limiting thoughts and emotions. But to do this, you will be required to reverse your senses. You may feel one thing, but you can choose to think something else.

The most challenging negative emotion I experience is despair. At times it just comes on like a wave and I don't seem to be able to stop the physical experience. Before I fully understood the core principles and practice of reversing your senses, during these experiences my thoughts would orchestrate a doomsday scenario for my life and/or circumstances. I could very easily have become extremely negative and critical of myself and others. My thoughts sounded something like this: "You are a loser; you don't deserve to be successful." "People don't care about you. They are selfish and they will take advantage of you if you don't protect yourself." But I began to observe my moods and thoughts, and through practice and discipline, I chose not to entertain those thoughts. Instead, I replaced them with my positive mantra and thus began to move through those periods more quickly. More importantly, during those periods I was less likely to reinforce the negative thoughts with my behavior.

The Power of Emotional Intelligence

It used to be that the leadership traits and skills we valued most were left-brain functions: intelligence, analysis, vision, focus. For most of the twentieth century, IQ was placed on a high pedestal and was considered to be one of the most important factors of success. This perspective was uprooted in 1995 when Daniel Goleman published his landmark book, *Emotional Intelligence: Why it Can Matter More than IQ*. He wrote, "At best, IQ contributes about 20 percent to the factors that determine life success, which leaves 80 percent to other forces." Primary among these "other forces" is emotional intelligence: "abilities such as being able to motivate oneself and persist in the face of frustrations; to control impulses and delay gratification; to regulate one's moods and keep distress from swamping the ability to think; to empathize and to hope."

In a January 2004 *Harvard Business Review* article entitled "What Makes a Leader," Goleman revealed that most effective leaders have a high degree of emotional intelligence. IQ and technical skills matter, he says, but only as basic requirements for executive positions. But without emotional intelligence, as the research shows, "a person can have the best training in the world, an incisive, analytical mind, and an endless supply of smart ideas, but he still won't make a great leader."

After performing exhaustive research with top executives, Goleman found that intellect was important for executive performance, including cognitive skills like big picture thinking and vision. But calculations proved emotional intelligence to be twice as important as other skills for jobs at all levels. Furthermore, the higher the company position, the more important emotional intelligence is to performance.

"When I compared star performers with average ones in senior leadership positions," Goleman wrote, "nearly 90 percent of the difference in their profiles was attributable to emotional intelligence factors rather than cognitive abilities."

According to Goleman, emotional intelligence includes five components:

1. Self-awareness: having a deep understanding of one's emotions, strengths, weaknesses, needs, and drives.
2. Self-regulation: Self-regulation, which is like an ongoing inner conversation, is the

component of emotional intelligence that frees us from being prisoners of our feelings. People engaged in such a conversation feel bad moods and emotional impulses just as everyone else does, but they find ways to control them and even to channel them in useful ways.

3. Motivation: Plenty of people are motivated by external factors, such as a big salary or the status that comes from having an impressive title or being part of a prestigious company. By contrast, those with leadership potential are motivated by a deeply embedded desire to achieve for the sake of achievement.

4. Empathy: For a leader, empathy means thoughtfully considering employees' feelings—along with other factors—in the process of making intelligent decisions.

5. Social skill: Social skill is friendliness with a purpose: moving people in the direction you desire, whether that's agreement on a new marketing strategy or enthusiasm about a new product.

One critical skill of emotional intelligence is the ability to override what Goleman calls "emotional hijacking," that is, a state in which we are jolted by some stimulus into "fight or flight" mode before our neocortex, or thinking brain, has a chance to make an accurate judgment. Essentially, emotional hijacking is when an emotional impulse overrides our rational thought processes. The more emotional intelligence we develop, the greater our ability to override emotional hijacking so we can reverse our senses—in this case, use our intellect to make wiser, more objective decisions.

The heart of all emotional matters in the brain is the amygdala, an almond-shaped cluster of interconnected structures located just above the brainstem and near the bottom of the limbic ring. "The amygdala," says Goleman, "acts as the storehouse of emotional memory, and thus of significance itself; life without the amygdala is a life stripped of personal meanings."

He continues by saying that

> The amygdala is poised something like an alarm company where operators stand ready to send out emergency calls to the fire department, police, and a neighbor whenever a home security system signals trouble. When it sounds an alarm of, say fear, it sends urgent messages to every major part of the brain: it triggers the secretion of the body's fight-or-flight hormones, mobilizes the centers for movement, and activates the cardiovascular system, the muscles, and the gut . . . The amygdala's extensive

web of neural connections allows it, during an emotional emergency, to capture and drive much of the rest of the brain—including the rational mind.

Clearly, there are situations in life that call for a fight or flight reaction, where we don't have time to sit and think through all the ramifications and consequences of each possible action. The challenge is that we can often perceive things as threats that don't, in fact, pose any legitimate threat. Thus, emotionally hijacked, we make impulsive decisions that we regret later.

The key to developing emotional intelligence is to practice self-awareness and other-awareness. Begin by becoming aware of the things in your world that trigger deep-seated emotions. When you are triggered, ask yourself the question: "What am I feeling and why?" You may not get answers initially, but over time you will experience being more tuned into your feeling and have a deeper sense of where these emotions are coming from.

By becoming more aware of our thought and emotional processes, we're better equipped to override disproportionate and inappropriate reactions from the amygdala's hypersensitivity. By developing our emotional intelligence, we're able to manage our thoughts and emotions better and think more clearly, act more sensibly, and make wiser decisions. In short, we're able to reverse our senses when needed.

Case Study: Abraham Lincoln

We know Abraham Lincoln as the heroic figure who led the United States through the Civil War, preserved the Union, and abolished slavery. He's the classic American success story—a self-educated frontiersman who, through hard work and grit, became a country lawyer and ultimately our sixteenth president.

What is often overlooked is that his accomplishments were overshadowed by the gloom of depression throughout his entire life. In his recent book, *Lincoln's Melancholy: How Depression Challenged a President and Fueled His Greatness*, Joshua Wolf Shenk details the scene of the 1860 state Republican convention in Decatur, Illinois. The crowd roared when Lincoln, fifty-one years old and at the peak of his political career, took the stage. Yet to the audience, Lincoln didn't seem pleased. One man observed, "I then thought him one of the most diffident and worst plagued men I ever saw."

When the crowds dispersed, writes Shenk, "The

lieutenant governor of Illinois, William J. Bross, walked the floor. He saw Lincoln sitting alone at the end of the hall, his head bowed, his gangly arms bent at the elbows, his hands pressed to his face. As Bross approached, Lincoln noticed him and said, 'I'm not very well.'"

Lincoln's look at that moment—the classic image of gloom—was familiar to everyone who knew him well. Such spells were just one thread in a curious fabric of behavior and thought that his friends called his "melancholy." He often wept in public and recited maudlin poetry. He told jokes and stories at odd times—he needed the laughs, he said, for his survival. As a young man, he talked more than once of suicide, and as he grew older, he said he saw the world as hard and grim, full of misery, made that way by fate and the forces of God. "No element of Mr. Lincoln's character," declared his colleague Henry Whitney, "was so marked, obvious and ingrained as his mysterious and profound melancholy." His law partner William Herndon said, "His melancholy dripped from him as he walked."

These weren't the first accounts of his depression. Mentor Graham, one of Lincoln's schoolteachers, said that as a young man Lincoln "told Me that he felt like

Committing Suicide often." In 1841, he wrote a letter to his law partner in which he stated, "I am now the most miserable man living. If what I feel were equally distributed to the whole human family, there would not be one cheerful face on the earth. Whether I shall ever be better I can not tell; I awfully forebode I shall not. To remain as I am is impossible; I must die or be better, it appears to me."

So, how did Lincoln overcome his depression to accomplish so much? Shenk explains that "he had an 'irrepressible desire' to accomplish something while he lived. He wanted to connect his name with the great events of his generation, and 'so impress himself upon them as to link his name with something that would redound to the interest of his fellow man.' This was no mere wish, Lincoln said, but what he 'desired to live for.'" In other words, his thoughts of making a difference were stronger and more prevalent than his depression.

"The mind is its own place, and in itself can make a heaven of hell, and a hell of heaven."

—JOHN MILTON

Although depression plagued him his whole life, Lincoln shows us that we don't have to be victims of our thoughts and emotions. We can reverse our senses and act with courage and achieve great things by making our thoughts stronger than our feelings about our circumstances. Most people will never experience clinical depression like Lincoln did. But if even he, with clinical depression, could overpower his emotions with his thoughts, anyone who experiences milder forms of negative thinking can as well.

As Lincoln himself put it, "Always bear in mind that your own resolution to success is more important than any other one thing."

CHAPTER 4

CORE PROCESS PRINCIPLE #3

MOST THOUGHTS AND EMOTIONS ARE SUBCONSCIOUS: AWARENESS IS THE FIRST STEP OF CHANGE

*"The better you know yourself, the better your
relationship with the rest of the world."*
—Toni Collette

INSCRIBED IN THE FORECOURT OF THE ANCIENT GREEK Temple of Apollo at Delphi was the phrase, "Gnothi Seauton." The phrase has been translated as "Know thyself." Benjamin Franklin admitted how hard it was to apply this advice when he wrote, "There are three things extremely hard: steel, a diamond, and to know one's self."

Through cognitive neuroscience, we now know why this advice is so hard to apply. We can't change what we don't know. And nowhere is this more true than our subconscious brain, from which springs thoughts, emotions, and actions that we're not even aware of.

According to Harvard professor Gerald Zaltman, 95 percent of our thoughts, emotions, and learning occur without our conscious awareness.

Most cognitive neuroscientists concur. Dr. A. K. Pradeep, the founder of NeuroFocus, a neuroscience research firm, estimates it at 99.999 percent.

Dan Ariely, professor of psychology and behavioral economics at Duke University and author of *Predictably Irrational: The Hidden Forces that Shape Our Decisions*, concludes from years of empirical research That "We are pawns in a game whose forces we largely fail to comprehend."

David Eagleman, neuroscientist at Baylor College of Medicine and author of *Incognito: The Secret Lives of the Brain*, writes: "Consciousness is the smallest player in the operations of the brain. Our brains run mostly on autopilot, and the conscious mind has little access to the giant and mysterious factory that runs below it."

Carl Jung expressed this concept simply when he said, "In each of us there is another whom we do not know."

And in the band Pink Floyd's song "Brain Damage" there's a line we can all relate to: "There's someone in my head but it's not me."

That someone is our subconscious brain, of which there are two components: The first component comprises the deepest levels of the brain, which monitor things like our breathing, heart rate, and muscle movement. That is essentially our biological machine, over which we have little to no control. The second component comprises the intuitive, visual, and emotional aspects of the right hemisphere of our brain, and learning to access, manage, and leverage this part is what matters to our success and happiness.

Our intuitive brain has access to knowledge that our left, conscious brain cannot even see. Intuition is our hunches, or gut feelings. Have you ever struggled with a business problem and felt a nagging sense that something was missing, or felt somehow drawn to a certain decision without being able to explain or articulate it? That's intuition. And by tapping into intuition, we see things that other people can't see; we connect dots and see patterns that we were previously blind to; and we make better decisions.

Unfortunately, our left, logical brain often prevents us from accessing the vast and unfathomable wisdom of our intuition. As Dr. R. Joseph writes in *The Right Brain and the Unconscious: Discovering the Stranger Within*, "Sometimes the left brain tries to dominate and tries to perform a task that is actually performed better by the right brain. In some instances, the left brain interferes with, suppresses, and inhibits right-brain mental processing so that its capacities and abilities are not expressed . . . Indeed, the left hemisphere may deny the significance of an intuitive conclusion drawn by the right half of the brain, even when someone is pointing it out."

Again, since our right, subconscious, intuitive brain can't speak to our left brain via language, it uses other ways to communicate. One way is through physical responses. Barnaby Dunn, PhD, a scientist at the Medical Research Council in the UK, conducted a study in which he measured how accurately subjects could count their heartbeats during timed intervals. Then he asked them to play a card game. They turned over cards from four different decks and won or lost money based on the cards they drew. Unbeknown to the subjects, the decks were rigged: Two had more high-value cards, and two were stacked with losers. As the subjects played, a sensor recorded changes in their heartbeats. After just a few rounds, the monitor showed a dip in players' heart rates whenever they went near certain decks. Dunn found that some individuals who'd been better able to measure their own heart rates performed better in the game overall. In other words, their intuition had picked up on how to win the game without them ever becoming consciously aware of what was happening. Their intuition manifested as a physical response.

A similar study performed at the University of Iowa measured the perspiration on players' palms. What they found is that within ten cards, players started getting sweatier palms. Yet they didn't become consciously aware that the decks were rigged until they'd turned over about fifty cards, and they weren't able to fully explain how the decks were stacked until they'd turned over eighty cards. Their sweaty hands were manifesting a subconscious intuition long before their conscious minds made the connection. (Interested readers will find more details about the study online at http://www.sciencedaily.com /releases/2011/01/110104114307.htm.)

Now get this: A 2005 study led by researchers at Massachusetts General Hospital (the results of which were published in *Psychiatry Research: Neuroimaging* in an article titled "Mindfulness practice leads to increases in regional brain gray matter density") revealed that in meditators, brain regions associated with sensitivity to the body's signals and sensory processing had more gray matter. (Interested readers will find more details about the study online at http://www.sciencedaily .com/releases/2011/01/110121144007.htm.)

The greater the meditation experience, the more developed the brain regions. In other words, the positive effects of meditation are more than emotional; they are physiological as well. Meditation not only helps you control your emotional responses but also actually changes your brain.

Our left-brain logical thought processes are slow and methodical, while our right-brain intuitive connections and insights are made quickly. And, as Ap Dijksterhuis, a psychologist at Radboud University in the Netherlands, discovered, our intuitive brain gnaws on problems nonstop, even after we consciously turn our attention to a different task. In one study, he asked subjects to evaluate four models of cars based on twelve variables. He found that only about 25 percent of those who were given uninterrupted time to ponder their choice opted for the best model, compared with 60 percent of people who were asked to make a spontaneous decision after looking over the cars and then performing another task. "While they were focusing on something else, the unconscious mind was processing the information and integrating it into a valid selection," Dijksterhuis explains.

One way to make better, more intuitive decisions, therefore, is to study a problem logically for a while, then stop and concentrate on other things. Thereafter, go with the first solution that comes to you. Pausing your conscious analysis gives your unconscious mind the bandwidth it needs to filter through the information and come up with the right answer.

Also, remember that our subconscious brain never sleeps, which is why we often come up with solutions while we sleep and through dreams. In 2004 neuroscientists Ullrich Wagner and Jan Born published in the journal *Nature* the results of a study that examined the relationship between sleep and problem solving. They gave participants a series of math problems, which required them to apply a set of tough algorithms.

However, they integrated an elegant shortcut into the problems that made the task easier. One group of participants wrestled with the problems for several hours only. A second group was allowed to work with the series of problems and then sleep on it. Researchers found that only 20 percent of the participants in the first group discovered the shortcut. Among the participants in the second group (the "sleepers," if you will) an astounding 60 percent of them discovered the shortcut. The researchers concluded that sleeping and dreaming "facilitates extraction of explicit knowledge and insightful behavior."

Vince Poscente wrote an excellent parable entitled *The Ant and the Elephant*, wherein he explains this phenomenon. "Our minds function in two distinct spaces—conscious and subconscious thought. Our 'ant' is the intentional part of the brain—it houses our critical, analytical thoughts. Our 'elephant,' however, is the instinctual, impulsive part of the brain—it houses emotions and memories and even guides the body to perform its vital functions. While we tend to know our conscious minds—or *ants*—rather well, we often overlook the power of our *elephantine* subconscious minds.

Unfortunately, when we do, we squander a wellspring of human potential."

One of the best techniques I know of for quieting our "ant" brain and accessing the awesome power of our "elephant" brain is meditation. You may balk at that word, and I don't blame you. It may seem like a "soft" concept in the "hard" world of business. Many of my clients initially struggle with its relevance to their lives, but they quickly learn how powerful it can be.

So let's keep this really simple and practical. Let's just call it "personal reflection." But no matter what name we give to this practice, I'm not talking about anything mystical, complicated, or even spiritual. I'm simply talking about sitting still for a few minutes each day, breathing deeply and allowing yourself to be present. Letting your mind wander until you connect with the "observer" of your thoughts. Watching the cluttered stream of your left-brain thoughts flow by while you tap into your deeper, intuitive self.

Quiet personal reflection creates greater awareness of your thoughts and emotions. It helps you to see things in a different way. It has a calming effect and relieves stress and frustration. In that space, you can make decisions with greater clarity and think more positively, creatively, and productively. It brings greater harmony between the right and the left hemispheres of your brain, which are often, if not usually, at odds with each other.

"Your vision will become clear only when you can look into your own heart . . . Who looks outside, dreams; who looks inside, awakes."

—CARL JUNG

Most important, it creates space for you to choose and to act proactively rather than reactively—to widen the gap between stimulus and response. In his great book *Ownership Spirit*, motivational speaker and corporate trainer Dennis Deaton teaches,

> Between stimulus and response we experience a mental interpretive gap. In that gap, we make choices; and in those moments of choice, the juice of life is squeezed . . . Without awareness, the gap between stimulus and response narrows to the point that it seems to vanish altogether. When that happens, our responses become fairly mechanical and predictable—just a series of conditioned responses to the routine flow of repeated stimuli,

and we become unwitting victims of our habits. When we are mindful of the gap, however, and pause for a split-second consideration, we widen the gap and that begets options. We then see a spectrum of choices, and usually opt for something better.

For example, suppose a business partner were to call you and unfairly accuse you of wrongdoing. The typical, immediate instinctive response would be to get defensive and angry and to fight back. But with awareness of the gap between stimulus and response, you can think through the consequences of such a response. You can consider different and better responses. You might wonder what's going on in his life that led to the outburst. Rather than being a victim or a slave of reaction, you could respond nondefensively and kindly. You could ask your business partner to help you understand his position better.

In such a situation, you would probably be surprised at how quickly a wise, kind, and proactive response would diffuse the situation. As the proverb says, "A soft answer turneth away wrath." Even if the partner who accused you is still angry, you'll at least feel better about having maintained control in the situation.

Or perhaps something goes wrong in your business. A supplier doesn't come through and leaves you hanging. When you find out, you have a moment of choice—Deaton's "mental interpretive gap." You could choose to interpret the supplier's failure as a sign of incompetence, sloppy work, or perhaps even deception. Or you could choose to interpret the event as something that happened beyond their control. In reality, it doesn't matter what the true reason; what matters is how you respond. The typical "victim" reaction—anger, threats, withdrawal—will do nothing to solve the situation. A more conscious and proactive response could turn a bad situation into something positive.

Novelist David Foster Wallace gave the commencement speech at Kenyon College in 2005. His speech, entitled "This Is Water," adds powerful insights into this principle of widening the gap between stimulus and response. He says that our default setting is to believe we're the center of the universe. He then gives an example of this kind of self-centered, default living. On a typical day, he says, you go to your job and work hard for eight to ten hours. After your workday, you're tired and stressed and you just want to go home and eat and unwind. But you have to stop at the grocery store on the way home. The supermarket is crowded: the crowds and the long checkout lines annoy you.

During times like this, he says, "If I don't make a conscious decision about how to think and what to pay attention to, I'm gonna be pissed and miserable every time I have to shop. Because my natural default setting is the certainty that situations like this are really all about me. About MY hungriness and MY fatigue and MY desire to just get home, and it's going to seem for all the world like everybody else is just in my way . . . Thinking this way tends to be so easy and automatic that it doesn't have to be a choice. It is my natural default setting. It's the automatic way that I experience the boring, frustrating, crowded parts of adult life when I'm operating on the automatic, unconscious belief that I am the center of the world, and that my immediate needs and feelings are what should determine the world's priorities."

But we don't have to think this way. We don't have to operate on this default setting. We can consciously choose to think more positively in moments like this. As Wallace puts it, "I can choose to force myself to consider the likelihood that everyone else in the supermarket's checkout line is just as bored and frustrated as I am, and that some of these people probably have harder, more tedious and painful lives than I do."

Snapping yourself out of default mode is critical, he says, because "If you're automatically sure that you know what reality is, and you are operating on your default setting, then you, like me, probably won't consider possibilities that aren't annoying and miserable. But if you really learn how to pay attention, then you will know there are other options. It will actually be within your power to experience a crowded, hot, slow, consumer-hell type situation as not only meaningful, but sacred . . ."

Personal reflection helps us to change our natural default setting to a heightened state of awareness and consideration. It helps us conquer instinctual negative reactions and to become more proactive. In our reflection time, we can consider how we've thought, felt, and acted in past experiences and how we could have reacted differently. This then carries forward into how we act in the future.

Consistent personal reflection can also help us to break deeply embedded negative habits that may be dragging us down. In his recent book, *The Power of Habit*, Charles Duhigg, a Pulitzer prize–winning reporter for the *New York Times*, details the science behind how habits form and how to change them. He explains that close to the center of our skull lies a golf-ball-sized lump of tissue called the basal ganglia, which has the job of storing habits even while the rest of our brain goes to sleep. Science has proven that repeated habits become ingrained into our basal ganglia forever.

Our brain is programmed to constantly find new ways to save effort. Writes Duhigg,

> Left to its own devices, the brain will try to make almost any routine into a habit, because habits allow our minds to ramp down more often . . . This process within our brains is a three-step loop. First, there is a cue, a trigger that tells your brain to go into automatic mode and which habit to use. Then there is the routine, which can be physical or mental or emotional. Finally, there is a reward, which helps your brain figure out if this particular loop is worth remembering for the future. Over time, this loop—cue, routine, reward; cue, routine, reward—becomes more and more automatic. The cue and reward become intertwined until a powerful sense of anticipation and craving emerges. Eventually . . . a habit is born.

Once born, no habit will ever die. As MIT scientist Ann Graybiel says, "Habits never really disappear. They're encoded into the structures of our brain, and that's a huge advantage for us, because it would be awful if we had to relearn how to drive after every vacation. The problem is that your brain can't tell the difference between bad and good habits, and so if you have a bad one, it's always lurking there, waiting for the right cues and rewards."

Habits exert enormous power over our brains and decision-making abilities. To quote Duhigg's explanation: "When a habit emerges, the brain stops fully participating in decision making. It stops working so hard, or diverts focus to other tasks. So unless you deliberately fight a habit—unless you find new routines—the pattern will unfold automatically."

Once again, personal reflection is a powerful way to become more aware of our decisions, to get the brain "participating" in decisions where previous habits may have shut it down.

And when we make personal reflection a "keystone habit" in our lives, the results over time can be astounding. Keystone habits, according to Duhigg, are seemingly small and simple habits, but ones that can catalyze a ripple effect and have a major impact on every aspect of your life. One proven example of this is exercise. "When people start habitually exercising, even as infrequently as once a week," writes Duhigg, "they start changing other, unrelated patterns in their lives, often unknowingly. Typically, people who exercise start eating better and becoming more productive at work. They smoke less and show more patience with colleagues and family. They use their credit cards less frequently and say they feel less stressed. It's not completely clear why. But for many people, exercise is a keystone habit that triggers widespread change."

From personal experience over years, I know that consistent personal reflection has a similar effect. It makes me less stressed, frustrated, and reactive. It gives me greater clarity and makes me more aware of the thoughts, emotions, and motivations behind my choices. It makes me more kind and patient in relationships. In short, I know of few other ways to dramatically improve all my life's results. And the beauty of it is that it's incredibly simple to do. Not *easy*, but simple, as you'll discover. But remember, just like exercise, you will receive no benefit unless you actually practice!

Case Study: Nelson Mandela

Nelson Mandela has always been one of my personal heroes, and his story fascinates me.

Born under the oppression and injustice of apartheid in South Africa, Mandela was deeply committed to freedom and equality. He joined the African National Congress (ANC) at age twenty-four, and for the next twenty years he directed peaceful, nonviolent acts of defiance against the South African government and its racist policies. He also cofounded a law firm and provided free and low-cost legal counsel to unrepresented blacks.

He had been an advocate of nonviolent resistance, but that changed in 1961 as he began to believe that armed struggle was the only way to achieve change. He subsequently cofounded Umkhonto we Sizwe, also known as MK, an armed offshoot of the ANC dedicated to sabotage and guerilla war tactics to end apartheid. After orchestrating a three-day national workers' strike, he was sentenced to five years in prison. Then, in 1963, he was brought to trial again. This time, he and other ANC leaders were sentenced to life imprisonment for political offenses.

Thus began an almost unfathomably long twenty-seven years of imprisonment. Imagine trying to manage your thoughts and emotions in that environment. Here in the free world, the issues we struggle with are so petty compared to Mandela's struggle.

Of course, we know the rest of the story: Mandela emerged from prison in 1991, as elected president of the ANC, and continued working toward an apartheid-free South Africa. He negotiated with President F. W. de Klerk to establish the country's first multiracial elections. Mandela rode a fine line, striving to strike a delicate balance between entrenched powers as well as forces within his own camp who wanted a complete transfer of power.

In 1993, Mandela and President de Klerk were jointly awarded the Nobel Peace Prize for their work toward dismantling apartheid. On April 27, 1994, South Africa held its first democratic elections. Nelson Mandela was inaugurated as the country's first black president on May 10, 1994, at the age of seventy-seven, with de Klerk as his first deputy. Mandela's work as president for the next five years required masterful statesmanship. He eased race relationships, improved the nation's economy, and established a new constitution, which was based on majority rule and guaranteed the rights of minorities and the freedom of expression.

What had happened during his twenty-seven years of imprisonment to give him the personal power to accomplish his goals and achieve his incredibly ambitious vision? Certainly, many forces were at play, yet in *Mandela: The Authorized Biography*, by Anthony Sampson, we find this revealing passage from Mandela himself:

> You may find that the cell is an ideal place to learn to know yourself, to search realistically and regularly the processes of your own mind and feelings. In judging our progress as individuals we tend to concentrate on external factors such as one's social position, influence and popularity, wealth and standard of education . . . But internal factors may be even more crucial in assessing one's development as a human being: honesty, sincerity, simplicity, humility, purity, generosity, absence of vanity, readiness to serve your fellow men—qualities within the reach of every soul—are the foundation of one's spiritual life . . . At least, if for nothing else, the cell gives you the opportunity to look daily into your entire conduct to overcome the bad and develop whatever is good in you. **Regular meditation, say of about fifteen minutes a day before you turn in, can be fruitful in this regard** [emphasis added]. You may find it

difficult at first to pinpoint the negative factors in your life, but the tenth attempt may reap rich rewards. Never forget that a saint is a sinner that keeps on trying.

As Mandela demonstrates, reversing the senses is not an easy or an immediate process. It takes time to cultivate the habits and disciplines that, in turn, change our perceptions and reactions. You may not see an immediate benefit from meditation. You may do it every day for thirty days and feel like it's pointless. But I guarantee that if you stick with it, eventually your life will start to change for the better. You'll start seeing things differently. You'll feel more courageous, more empowered, more at peace.

Nelson Mandela, one of the greatest statesmen and most accomplished men in history, used meditation to overcome personal limitations and achieve his goals. He had twenty-seven years to apply the ancient Greek advice, "Know thyself."

The fantastic news? You don't need decades of imprisonment to do the same. Through consistent, daily personal reflection, you too can come to know yourself. You can become aware of the subconscious forces behind your thoughts and emotions. And that can make all the difference to your ultimate success.

CHAPTER 5

CORE PROCESS PRINCIPLE #4

TRUE SUCCESS IS INTERNAL HARMONY

"Men do not attract that which they want, but that which they are."
—James Allen

AS I MENTIONED IN THE INTRODUCTION, IT IS ONE OF life's great ironies that the highest achievers are often the most discontent. Those who seem to have the most success by the world's standards—wealth, status, prestige, credentials—often feel like they can never achieve enough to fill the void they feel inside.

This is not a criticism: it was the story of much of my life. I get it. It's not a character flaw to feel guilty about. It's simply something to be aware of and to deal with so that you can be happier, more peaceful, and more productive.

This constant feeling of dissatisfaction is the product of what I call "high achiever's syndrome," where a person associates love with success. This is particularly dangerous and hard to uproot when that association is made at an early age. You can never achieve enough. You always need external praise to fuel your drive, while you're slowly dying inside. You vacillate between feeling great and feeling like you're dying *depending on what the world gives you.*

As with all five of the Core Process principles, the solution is to turn away from the world and to turn inward. The first step is to redefine success. Money, cars, a thriving business, vacations, a front row parking space—these are merely *byproducts* of success. They are evidence of achievement, but they are not success itself.

True success is internal harmony—feeling comfortable in your own skin.

> *"Attitude, to me, is more important . . . than the past . . . than money, than circumstances, than failures, than successes, than what other people think or say or do. It is more important than appearance, giftedness, or skill. It will make or break a company, a church, a home. The remarkable thing is we have a choice every day regarding the attitude we will embrace for that day."*
>
> —CHARLES SWINDOLL

The more your inner thoughts and feelings align with how you present yourself to the external world, the more at peace you will be. The converse is also true. My client Dan was a walking billboard for the latter.

Dan is a very successful and accomplished CEO who prides himself on being prepared and on top of things. Unfortunately, what was driving him was a deep-seated uneasiness with who he really was. His inner thoughts and feelings about not being good enough and being found out drove him to overprepare for everything. In this state, he wouldn't enter into any experience or environment that he felt he couldn't control.

This conflict came to a head when the company he was running tripled in size after a major acquisition. The adjustment was far greater than Dan had anticipated, and his lack of internal harmony was soon apparent to everyone around him. One minute Dan was the calm and cool professional his staff had come to respect and admire, the next he was angry, combative, and downright irrational.

After I spent some time with Dan, it became apparent that his internal world was in complete disarray. The acquisition was just the tipping point for years of living a life that demanded complete external control to protect his internal thoughts and emotions. Once Dan began to realize what he had been doing and why, the conflict subsided, the fear and emotional outbursts were reduced, and his ability to let go of control increased dramatically.

In Dan's case, the recognition of his internal conflict was realized as he began to explore his life as a child. He began to see a consistent theme between how he felt and acted when he experienced disapproval from his parents, and, as he got older, from anyone in a position of authority. Through the process of self-awareness, he began to make better sense of his emotions and to become less reactive to their effects on his thoughts about himself.

Dan learned, as is true for all of us, that once we can truly begin to see the conflict we experience internally and begin to resolve this conflict, our external world becomes less threatening and we feel less of a need to control every aspect to protect ourselves from being "found out."

In the New Testament, Jesus asks, "For what is a man profited, if he shall gain the whole world, and lose his own soul? Or what shall a man give in exchange for his soul?" Remove the religious connotation from this thought and think of it in relation to high achiever's syndrome. What good does all the material wealth and external success in the world do for us if we don't have internal harmony? Can money ever replace a deep and abiding sense of satisfaction, inner peace, and happiness? If we define success by external factors, by definition we can never be successful because it can never be enough.

"What lies behind us and what lies before us are tiny matters compared to what lies within us."

—RALPH WALDO EMERSON

The Danger of Comparison

Defining success by external factors leads to comparison. It doesn't matter how much money we have—there will always be someone with more. It doesn't matter how nice our car is—there will always be someone with a nicer, more expensive one. Knowing that is like a splinter in our souls, constantly festering.

Virtually every self-help and success book you'll find includes the imperative to set goals. Failure, therefore, is defined as not reaching one's goals. As Dr. William Menninger, a psychiatrist famous for treating behavioral disorders, said, "A fellow must know where he wants to go, if he is going to get anywhere. The people who go places and do things . . . know what they want and are willing to go an extra mile." Or as Mark Twain quipped, "I can teach anybody how to get what they want out of life. The problem is that I can't find anybody who can tell me what they want."

Certainly, defining what we want—our goals—is fundamental to success. But even more fundamental is knowing *why* we want those goals. In short, the first step of true success is not setting goals but rather clearly and authentically defining success for ourselves. Achieving inauthentic goals does not constitute success. In fact, it's usually a more tragic failure than not achieving the right goals for the right reasons.

Our goals, particularly for high achievers, can often be misguided. We can be driven by praise or by the discontentment fostered by comparison or the desire to prove naysayers wrong—all of which are external factors. They can never give us the satisfaction we crave.

Stephen R. Covey put it this way: "It's incredibly easy to get caught up in an activity trap, in the business of life, to work harder and harder at climbing the ladder of success only to discover it's leaning against the wrong wall." External factors are the wrong wall. It's why we never feel satisfied even after climbing to the top.

Worthy goals can only be determined after we've defined success *for ourselves individually*. Our definition of success determines which goals are worthy of our purpose and which are misguided, inauthentic distractions. Any time we change our definition of success, the goals we pursue and how we achieve them also change drastically.

All too often we feel like failures when we compare ourselves to others. But this feeling does not come because we haven't achieved the same goals as other people. Rather, it comes because we've failed to define our own success and have bought into *their* definition. Envy is the result of not being in tune with who we are, what we were born to accomplish, our true purpose. Envy dissolves when we define success for ourselves based on an authentic understanding of our unique gifts, passions, values, and purpose.

Physical and holistic health guru Deepak Chopra has said, "Success in life could be defined as the continued expansion of happiness and the progressive realization of worthy goals." *Worthy* goals, mind you, as determined by your personal standard of success. With an internal compass of success, our only concern becomes how well we live up to our own standards. We can forget about what anyone else is doing and concentrate on being our best selves—being better today than we were yesterday. It's not about looking out the window trying to keep up with the Joneses; it's about looking in the mirror and living up to our own standards.

Even when we fall short of our standards, we must realize that happiness is a choice. As Helen Keller said, "Your success and happiness lies in you. Resolve to keep happy, and your joy shall form an invincible host against difficulties."

Examine and Fine-Tune Your Motivations

When I work with clients who struggle with internal harmony, I often invite them to examine their motivations. I know that's a critical area to explore because I was the master of being motivated by the wrong reasons. As I shared with you in the introduction, in high school I was driven by the desire to excel in sports in order to stay in the spotlight and receive praise. That misguided, external drive continued through college. In my early years of business, I was all about the money. My self-worth was largely determined by my net worth.

Drive and internal satisfaction are good things as long as they are not tied deeply to your sense of self-worth. Any drive other than doing what brings you internal satisfaction is like fireworks—it may give you lots of energy initially, but it will eventually fizzle out. It's not sustainable. It may drive you to achieve great things in business, but it will always leave you feeling dissatisfied. You'll always feel like you're missing something.

Money is great to have. But it should be put in its proper context—as the byproduct of value creation by following your passion and living your purpose. Having money and feeling happy, peaceful, and satisfied need not be mutually exclusive. But if you had to pick one or the other, which would it be?

It's also great to be recognized for making a contribution to the world. Yet nothing compares to the feeling of knowing you're doing things for the right reasons and staying true to your personal values.

For many people, doing the right thing and staying true to their values is the most challenging aspect of life. The Core Process is about focusing on principles that will ensure that you are able to internally know what is right. And once you are on that path, external course corrections become less difficult to manage. Instead of turning the *Titanic*, you are simply adjusting the rudder of your smooth-sailing dinghy.

I often encounter in my clients a deep fear—a fear of being discovered as a poser, a fear of never being adequate, a fear of failure, a fear of vulnerability. That deep-seated fear has actually driven them to a certain level of success, but eventually the fear fuel burns out and they come to me when they're running on fumes. Someone once said, "Don't be pushed by your fear, be pulled by your bliss." Albert Schweitzer conveyed the idea in these words: "Success is not the key to happiness. Happiness is the key to success." Success naturally follows when we do things that bring us joy.

When I help clients move away from fear and tap into their bliss, a whole new world opens up to them. For example, my client Betty had a very difficult childhood. Her parents divorced when she was a young girl, and their constant fighting and lack of attention to creating a stable home environment left her feeling alone. They were never around and did not seem to care much what she did. She was constantly being uprooted and pawned off from one parent to the other. This translated into a deep fear of being abandoned and left alone to fend for herself. What little relationship she had with her mother and her father was characterized by Betty desperately trying to gain each parent's approval, only to have them either dismiss her achievements or berate her for not doing even better.

As an adult, Betty became a very successful businesswoman. She connected with a small company whose owners were driven but caring, and they took Betty under their wing. Betty helped to transform that organization from a small mom-and-pop business into a large, well-respected, and highly profitable company.

When Betty sought me out, the founders of the company were in their eighties. Betty had been in charge for years, but she still felt the founders could pull the rug out from under her at any time. She found that this fear was hindering her ability to continue to grow the organization. This belief was not founded in reality, given the structure of the organization. It was apparent that Betty was in charge and the founders could not change that fact.

In addressing this situation, Betty had to confront where her fears were really coming from. Through six months of personal exploration of her past, she began to see clearly that her internal messaging was designed to protect her from the fear of being abandoned. She began to understand that the destructive thoughts and feelings she was experiencing were not based in the reality of her circumstances. Once she could see this clearly, the practice of thought and emotion observation (self-awareness and reduction of negative self-talk) combined with autosuggestion techniques (specifically telling herself that she was not alone and that she was lovable) assisted her in moving beyond her triggers and to move the company forward.

The practice of moving beyond subconscious fear is an extremely challenging one because in most cases you are unaware of where the fear is coming from. Your experience is very real, however, and your thoughts regarding how to protect yourself seem very logical.

In Betty's case, she was able to reverse her own senses regarding how she felt and thought and to create a new reality for herself. Once she was able to do this she began to apply this principle in other areas of her life and realize the incredible internal freedom that it produces.

Once you begin to experience the effects of applying the Core Process, all of life takes on a new perspective. Remember, wherever you go, there you are!

Integrity: Staying True to Yourself

In my business career, I've often felt tension between my personal values and integrity and doing what seemed to be necessary to "win." Prior to committing myself to the principles that I live my life by today, there always seemed to be a lot of gray area in business, especially when winning was on the line. Remember that for me achievement was deeply associated at a subconscious level with love, and winning in business meant you hit your numbers come hell or high water!

One time in particular I recall having a disastrous quarter as we were preparing for the sale of our business. These results could have potentially derailed the deal, and I knew in my heart of hearts that they were not indicative of the company's future viability. I wrestled endlessly with the thought of what this might do not only to myself but also to the other stakeholders in the business. My emotions were running high and my thoughts were spinning from one scenario to the next.

*"It's not hard to make decisions when
you know what your values are."*

—ROY DISNEY

Ultimately I made the decision not to manipulate
the numbers and/or cover up the reality of what we
were experiencing in the business. At this time, I had
not been practicing the Core Process principles, so my
choice was instinctive, but with conflict. Clearly, it was
the right decision, but the emotional toll it took on
me could have been avoided if I had had the internal capacity to eliminate the fear and to trust that the
only course was to do what was right. There would have
been no second option to consider. In the end we did
sell the business, to the same buyer, at a premium. It
just took a little longer to get it done.

High achievers tend to be extremely competitive,
which can make justification easier. From the vantage
point of my experience, justification usually comes in the
form of treating others unkindly or being self-centered.
But it can sometimes also cross the line and cause us to
do things that are blatantly unethical. I'm certain that

the only way Kenneth Lay and Bernie Madoff were able to live with their lies over the course of years and years was by self-justification. When they were in the middle of bilking investors, I doubt they thought of themselves as we see them—narcissistic and even evil.

"He that will do the least sin against conscience is prepared in disposition to do the greatest."

—LORD ACTON

But in the end, however minor our justifications, the slightest deficiency of integrity catches up with us, if only in the form of bad feelings. Being true to our values and ethical standards is a critical component of internal harmony. As Stephen R. Covey said, "As you live your values, your sense of identity, integrity, control, and inner-directedness will infuse you with both exhilaration and peace. You will define yourself from within, rather than by people's opinions or by comparisons to others. 'Wrong' and 'right' will have little to do with being found out."

"Happiness is when what you think, what you say, and what you do are in harmony."

—MAHATMA GANDHI

The Power of Gratitude

It may sound simplistic, but I know of few other ways to overcome anger, frustration, and stress than to simply count our blessings. Things are never as bad as they seem, and they can always get worse. When we feel dissatisfied, oftentimes it's because we're focused on everything that's wrong in our life. A simple readjustment of focus onto all of the amazing blessings we enjoy can make all the difference.

Seriously, take ten minutes right now to consciously count your blessings. Ponder what your life would be without each. Watch what happens to your mindset and feelings as a result.

One of the most powerful examples of gratitude I've found is in Corrie ten Boom's book, *The Hiding*

Place. Corrie and her sister, Betsie, were Dutch citizens during World War II. After hiding Jews in their home, they were arrested by Nazis and transported to a female extermination camp in Germany. They were marched to their barracks where they found the bedding crawling with fleas.

Imprisoned, hungry, and suffering, the sisters turned to the Bible to find strength. They read a passage in 1 Thessalonians that said, "Rejoice always, pray constantly, give thanks in all circumstances . . ."

To Corrie's surprise, Betsie immediately began praying and said, "Thank You for the fleas."

Corrie interjected, "Betsie, there's no way even God can make me grateful for a flea."

"Give thanks in all circumstances," Betsie quoted. "It doesn't say, 'in pleasant circumstances.'"

Days went by and they found that they had more freedom in their barracks than was expected. One day Betsie told Corrie, "You know we've never understood why we had so much freedom in the big room. Well, I've found out."

That afternoon, Betsie said, there'd been confusion in her knitting group about sock sizes and they'd asked the supervisor to come and settle it.

"But she wouldn't," said Betsie. "She wouldn't step through the door and neither would the guards. And you know why? Because of the fleas! That's what she said, 'That place is crawling with fleas!'"

It was then that Corrie remembered Betsie's prayer thanking God for the fleas, and understood how she could find reasons to be grateful in the worst imaginable circumstances.

There's always something to be grateful for, and by focusing on our blessings we're much more inclined to be happy and peaceful, as evidenced by the studies I referenced earlier.

Move from Financial Success to Significance

Thought leader and author Roy H. Williams says that everyone wants to make the same three things: money, a name, and a difference. How we prioritize the three is what creates diversity in human action. Social entrepreneur and venture philanthropist Bob Buford says, "The first half of life is a quest for success, the second is a quest for significance." Roy H. Williams adds,

"Success is measured by the money and the name you've made. Significance is measured by the difference you've made."

For some of my readers, you may want to shift your life focus from success to significance to find the internal harmony you seek. This is not to say that your business success has not made a difference—it absolutely has. But after achieving it, you may be ready to move to a different level in life. Gandhi says that "Our greatness lies not so much in being able to remake the world as in being able to remake ourselves." By "remaking" yourself, or at least shifting your focus, at this stage in your life, you can have a much greater impact on the world. And as you do so, your internal harmony will increase.

"You are not here merely to make a living. You are here to enable the world to live more amply, with greater vision, and with a finer spirit of hope and achievement. You are here to enrich the world. You impoverish yourself if you forget this errand."

—WOODROW WILSON

Perhaps there's a charity you've always wanted to start or an existing one you've wanted to support? Or could it be a school or a mentoring program? How can you leverage your wealth and success to alleviate suffering and make the world a better place? What great cause do you feel inspired to promote?

Consider the perspective taught by Viktor Frankl, the world-changing psychiatrist and Nazi concentration camp survivor, in his book *Man's Search for Meaning*:

> Don't aim at success. The more you aim at it and make it a target, the more you are going to miss it. For success, like happiness, cannot be pursued; it must ensue, and it only does so as the unintended side effect of one's personal dedication to a cause greater than oneself or as the by-product of one's surrender to a person other than oneself. Happiness must happen, and the same holds for success: you have to let it happen by not caring about it. I want you to listen to what your conscience commands you to do and go on to carry it out to the best of your knowledge. Then you will live to see that in the long-run—in the long-run, I say!—success will follow you precisely because you had forgotten to think about it.

I have been a member of the Young Presidents Organization (YPO) for many years. YPO is an international organization whose members are CEOs of mid- to larger-sized companies. The purpose of YPO is to provide a place where the leaders of these organizations can come together to share ideas, increase their knowledge, and learn from one another in a confidential environment.

As a result of my affiliation with YPO, I have had the opportunity to develop many relationships with CEOs from around the world and to see firsthand the challenges that accompany holding the top job in an organization. I have also witnessed the transition that many face when they have reached the point of ultimate financial security and are now left to ponder what to do with the rest of their lives. For many, this is not a question of what they'll do in old age, but what they'll do for the next thirty or forty years.

"What you leave behind is not what is engraved in stone monuments, but what is woven into the lives of others."

—PERICLES

One good friend of mine made this transition better than most, and his story highlights the importance of developing the internal capacity to move from financial success to significance. Mark was and is a very successful leader in the commercial real estate industry. His keen eye for seeing future trends in the market, combined with his tireless and focused effort, resulted in him being able to retire at age forty-eight. During the final stages of managing his business, he began to ponder much bigger questions regarding life and what was truly important.

He began to take stock of himself and his own internal struggles. Today he focuses his energy and tremendous talent on helping nonprofits develop sustainable models so they are less reliant on donations to survive and thrive. He also started a global publication and network called "Real Leaders" that focuses on inspiring better leaders for a better world. His passion centers on assisting others in moving from "money to meaning" in their lives and making a difference for good.

Mark's successful transition did not just happen. He *made* it happen, and he started with himself through the process of developing his own internal capacity and extending his new thoughts, ideas, and influence to the world around him. He now works harder than he ever has, but he would be the first to tell you that the greatest gift he has received is the internal harmony that he experiences as a result of his internal and external worlds being more in alignment.

"Be ashamed to die until you have won some victory for humanity."

—HORACE MANN

Could it be time for you to dedicate yourself to a great cause? If so, start from the inside out!

Case Study: Richard Branson

Founder and chairman of the Virgin Group of more than four hundred companies and the fourth richest citizen of the United Kingdom (his estimated net worth is $4.2 billion), Richard Branson is a consummate high achiever. He's the only entrepreneur to have built eight separate billion-dollar companies in eight different industries—and he did it all without a degree in business.

Branson started his first business venture, a magazine called *Student*, at the age of sixteen. Six years later, in 1972, he opened his first chain of record stores, Virgin Records. His Virgin brand skyrocketed, propelling him to launch Virgin Atlantic Airways in 1984. His most recent venture is Virgin Galactic, a space tourism company.

Branson is also known for his sporting achievements, notably the record-breaking Atlantic crossing in Virgin *Atlantic Challenger II* in 1986, and the first crossing by hot-air balloon of the Atlantic (1987) and the Pacific (1991). He was knighted in 1999 for his contribution to entrepreneurship.

So, what can he teach high achievers about true success and internal harmony? First of all, his cardinal rule is to never do anything that he doesn't enjoy. In his book *Like a Virgin: Secrets They Won't Teach You at Business School*, he writes, "When I started Virgin from a basement in west London, there was no great plan or strategy. I didn't set out to build a business empire . . . For me, building a business is all about doing something to be proud of, bringing talented people together and creating something that's going to make a real difference to other people's lives."

Is money the best motivator? Not according to Branson. "Above all, you want to create something you're proud of. This has always been my philosophy of business. I can honestly say that I have never gone into any business purely to make money. If that is the sole motive, then I believe you are better off not doing it." In an article in *Entrepreneur* magazine entitled "Richard Branson: Five Secrets to Business Success," he said, "If a businessperson sets out to make a real difference to other people's lives, and achieves that, he or she will be able to pay the bills and have a successful business to boot."

What drives Sir Richard? "It is the satisfaction of doing it for yourself," he says, "and motivating others to work with you in bringing it about. It is about the fun, innovation, creativity with the rewards being far greater than purely financial." He adds in his autobiography, explaining his decision to start his airline, that "My interest in life comes from setting myself huge, apparently unachievable challenges and trying to rise above them . . . from the perspective of wanting to live life to the full, I felt that I had to attempt it."

What about making a difference and living with significance? Says Branson, "For a successful entrepreneur it can mean extreme wealth. But with extreme wealth comes extreme responsibility. And the responsibility for me is to invest in creating new businesses, create jobs, employ people, and to put money aside to tackle issues where we can make a difference." In addition to his successful business ventures, Branson has also made a name for himself as a global humanitarian.

Finally, Branson confirms the necessity of defining success for ourselves. In an interview with Success magazine he said, "Entrepreneurship is business's beating heart. Entrepreneurship isn't about capital; it's about ideas. Entrepreneurship is also about excellence. Not excellence measured in awards or other people's approval, but the sort that one achieves for oneself by exploring what the world has to offer."

Take it from Richard Branson: Do what you love for the right reasons, stay true to yourself, strive to make a difference in the lives of others, live a life of meaning and significance, and you'll find internal harmony.

CHAPTER 6

CORE PROCESS PRINCIPLE #5

MANAGING YOUR THOUGHTS AND EMOTIONS INCREASES YOUR INTERNAL CAPACITY TO LEAD AND ACHIEVE

"Peace is inside you. Wherever you go, peace goes with you. When you climb on a bus, peace goes with you. When you are fighting, peace goes with you. When you are asleep, peace is within you. When you are frustrated beyond imagination, peace is in you. No matter what you do, there is no place you can go where peace will not come with you. Because it's within you. Through technology, we want to improve our lives. What I am saying is that the real improvement begins with you."
—Prem Rawat

IN THE INTRODUCTION, I MENTIONED BRIEFLY THAT people often search in the wrong ponds for answers to their questions, solutions to their problems, peace to calm their frustrations. By now it should be clear to you that the wrong ponds are anything outside yourself.

For high achievers, this usually takes the form of them searching for the right business strategy to break through their ceiling of limitations. They'll read books and attend seminars, listen to CDs and seek out mentors, ever grasping for tools and techniques, constantly fishing for new ideas in the wrong waters. The truth is that the right pond to fish in is their own soul. They carry their own answers, solutions, and peace inside themselves.

"We carry within us the wonders we seek without us."

—THOMAS BROWNE

Just as Michael Phelps increased his lung capacity through dedicated practice, going inside ourselves and learning to draw strength from our own internal resources, through personal reflection and other techniques, increases our capacity to reverse our senses and to lead and achieve. It's how we experience those moments where, like Oskar Schindler, we see the red coat. We experience a clarity that can be achieved through no other way, which shows us the right path to walk and the right actions to take.

I've had many moments of frustration and many tough decisions to make. There was none greater than when I was in transition from the last business I sold to contemplating what I would do for the rest of my life.

For me, the greatest red coat moment came when I reversed my own senses regarding how I felt about doing consulting work and my desire to do things that were interesting to me. I began to ask myself questions like these:

- How do you like to spend your time?
- What are the things you like to do on a daily basis?
- If you didn't care what other people thought, what would you do?

Addressing these questions led me down a path to begin exploring my own internal process. I pondered how my thoughts were being affected by how I felt, how my thoughts affected my experiences, and what would happen if I actually paid attention to this process. Ultimately, that process led me to do the work I am committed to today—and it is far different from what I could ever have imagined.

Once you are on the path of developing internal harmony, you will never go back. Fears and concerns regarding you and the future begin to disappear. Answers to life's challenges seem to come more easily with less effort. Your clarity of purpose begins to take shape and provides a solid foundation for sustainable achievement.

"The truth is that our finest moments are most likely to occur when we are feeling deeply uncomfortable, unhappy, or unfulfilled. For it is only in such moments, propelled by our discomfort, that we are likely to step out of our ruts and start searching for different ways or truer answers."

—M. SCOTT PECK

Today I have a thriving consulting practice through which I assist business leaders in developing and applying the principles I discuss in this book to themselves and their organizations. I also manage investments that focus on products and/or services that relate to the development and application of these principles. The guiding principles I live by today are not so much based on what I do as on who I am becoming.

My clients, and high achievers in general, are doers and hard workers. They wouldn't have gotten to where they are without having the courage to take action, the drive to take initiative. So when I suggest that personal reflection, or meditation, may be useful for them, they usually don't get it at first. They're looking for advice on what they should *do* to overcome their challenges.

I respond that meditation *is* doing something—and probably one of the hardest things anyone can do. I tell them that they are the experts about their business and they have the answers. They just have to find them and fish them up from their subconscious mind.

> *"Isn't it true that the realities of the inner life seem like marvels only because we live so far away from them?"*
>
> —JACQUES LUSSEYRAN

To know what to do, we must first see clearly. And we can't see clearly if our minds are cluttered with random thoughts, buzzing with frustration, bogged down by doubt and worry. When we consistently take time for quiet personal reflection, all that junk drifts away and we enter an intuitive state where the most important things are clear. We see the red coat. We know what to do. We can act with confidence and power.

What We Focus on Grows

When one of my clients struggles with the concept of meditation, I make it really practical for them. I tell them that what we focus on grows. They've come to me because they've got a challenge they're trying to overcome, a problem they haven't been able to solve. In virtually every case, they've been focused so heavily on the problem, they're not able to see the solution.

If we want to discover a solution, the first step is to envision and focus on the desired outcome. What are you trying to make happen? What will your life and/or business look like when you've broken through your ceiling of limitations and achieved an ideal solution? What is your vision of the ideal outcome? Got it? Good. Now spend just fifteen minutes a day sitting quietly, reflecting on that vision. See it in minute detail. Let the emotions of what it will feel like when you achieve your vision flow through you.

This helps you release your worries. Your random thoughts drift away. The power of your mind is harnessed and channeled toward the achievement of your goal.

---

*"Cherish your vision and your dreams
as they are the children of your soul; the
blueprints of your ultimate achievements."*

—NAPOLEON HILL

Neuroplasticity: The Power to Rewire Our Brains

One of the most revolutionary and empowering insights coming from cutting-edge neuroscience is the fact that we can literally change our brains by thinking different thoughts. In her enlightening book *Train Your Mind, Change Your Brain*, Sharon Begley explains that the paradigm in the scientific community for the past few centuries is that the brain is essentially fixed, hardwired, unchangeable. This view was summed up by Santiago Ramón y Cajal, a Spanish neuroanatomist, when he said, "In the adult centers the nerve paths are something fixed, ended and immutable." In other words, as Begley summarized it, "the circuits of the living brain are unchanging, its structures and organizations almost as static and stationary as a deathly white cadaver floating in a vat of formaldehyde."

But study after study is changing this view to fit the facts. As Begley reports,

> The brain can indeed be rewired. It can expand the area that is wired to move the fingers, forging new connections that underpin the dexterity of an accomplished violinist. It can activate long-dormant wires and run new cables like an electrician bringing an old house up to code, so

that regions that once saw can instead feel or hear. It can quiet circuits that once crackled with the aberrant activity that characterizes depression and cut pathological connections that keep the brain in the oh-god-something-is-wrong state that marks obsessive-compulsive disorder. The adult brain, in short, retains much of the plasticity of the developing brain, including the power to repair damaged regions, to grow new neurons, to rezone regions that performed one task and have them assume a new task, to change the circuitry that weaves neurons into the networks that allow us to remember, feel, suffer, think, imagine, and dream.

In other words, it's not just that thinking positive thoughts helps us to feel better and have a better attitude. *Positive, productive thinking can actually change the biological structure of our brains.* Amazing! Begley continues, "Brain changes can be generated by pure mental activity . . . Something as seemingly insubstantial as thought has the ability to act back on the very stuff of the brain, altering neuronal connections in a way that can lead to recovery from mental illness and perhaps to a greater capacity for empathy and compassion."

*"I know of no more encouraging fact
than the unquestionable ability of man to
elevate his life by conscious endeavor."*

—HENRY DAVID THOREAU

And believe it or not, one of the best tools scientists have used to discover neuroplasticity is the practice of "mindfulness meditation," described by the Buddhist monk Nyanaponika Thera as "the clear and single-minded awareness of what actually happens to us and in us, at the successive moments of perception. It . . . attends just to the bare facts of a perception as presented either through the five physical senses or through the mind . . . without reacting to them by deed, speech, or by mental comment which may be one of self-reference (like, dislike, etc.), judgment or reflection."

In the late 1980s, UCLA neuropsychiatrist Jeffrey Schwartz experimented with mindfulness with his obsessive-compulsive disorder (OCD) patients. He hypothesized that mindfulness could make them aware that their obsessions were caused by malfunctions in their brain, not true signals of distress. "It seemed worth investigating whether learning to observe your sensations and thoughts with the calm clarity of an external witness could strengthen the capacity to resist the insistent thoughts of OCD," says Schwartz. "I felt that if I could get patients to experience the OCD symptoms without reacting emotionally to the discomfort it caused, realizing instead that even the most visceral OCD urge is actually no more than the manifestation of a brain wiring defect that has no reality in itself, it might be tremendously therapeutic."

Schwartz trained his patients to recognize obsessive thoughts and then think: "My brain is generating another obsessive thought. Don't I know it is not real but just some garbage thrown up by a faulty circuit?" The vast majority of his patients began reporting positive results within just one week. The research team performed PET scans before and after ten weeks of mindfulness-based therapy. For most of them, the final PET scans showed physical changes in their brains. "Therapy had altered the metabolism of the OCD circuit," Schwartz reported. "This was the first study to show that cognitive-behavior therapy has the power to systematically change faulty brain chemistry in a well-identified brain circuit." His ultimate conclusion was that "Mental action can alter the brain chemistry of an OCD patient. The mind can change the brain."

Schwartz also said, "Conscious thoughts and volitions can, and do, play a powerful causal role in the world, including influencing the activity in the brain. Willed mental activity can clearly and systematically alter brain function. The exertion of willful effort generates physical force that has the power to change how the brain works and even its physical structure. The result is directed neuroplasticity."

Mindfulness, or meditation, has also been proven to successfully treat depression. Cambridge University researcher John Teasdale suspected that depressed patients might suffer fewer relapses if they learned to regard depressive thoughts "simply as events in their mind," as he put it. Reporting on Teasdale's process, Begley explained that "the key would be to help patients become aware of their thoughts and relate to them merely as brain events rather than as absolute truths . . . instead of allowing their feeling to drag them down into the pit of depression, patients would learn to respond with 'Thoughts are not facts,' or 'I can watch this thought come and go without having to respond to it.'"

The researchers studied two groups: one group of subjects who were given mindfulness-based cognitive therapy, and another group of subjects who were given regular treatments. After eight weeks of the respective treatments, the scientists then followed the patients for an additional year. As Begley reported in *Train Your Mind, Change Your Brain*, regular treatment left "34 percent of the patients free of relapse." But with mindfulness-based therapy, "66 percent remained relapse-free." That translates into "a *44 percent reduction in the risk of relapse*" among those who received mindfulness-based cognitive therapy compared to those who received usual care.

I don't bring up these studies to suggest that you need treatment for some disorder. The point is that if mindfulness meditation can work on even extreme OCD and depressed patients, it can work for you. If it can rewire a brain with faulty chemistry, it can help you overcome your worry, fear, and anxiety. It can help you to identify and detach from negative thoughts and not internalize them. As you do so, you become more calm and confident. You're kinder to people and more sensitive to their needs. You make better decisions. In short, it can expand your capacity to lead and achieve.

> *"All men dream: but not equally. Those who dream by night in the dusty recesses of their minds wake in the day to find that it was vanity: but the dreamers of the day are dangerous men, for they may act their dream with open eyes, to make it possible."*
>
> —LAWRENCE OF ARABIA

By itself, thinking can even improve your technical skills, as proven by a study performed by Harvard neurology professor Alvaro Pascual-Leone. He taught a group of volunteers a five-finger exercise on a piano keyboard, instructing them to play as fluidly as possible, without pausing, and trying hard to keep to the metronome's sixty beats per minute. They practiced for two hours a day, every day, for five days. They then took a test where they played the exercise twenty times while a computer counted their errors. The test showed marked improvement over the five days. The players made fewer and fewer errors and came closer to keeping up with the metronome.

Pascual-Leone then used magnetic pulses to the

motor cortex of each subject's brain to map what was happening in their brain. After one week of practice, the researchers discovered the stretch of motor cortex devoted to these finger movements took over surrounding areas like "dandelions on a suburban lawn."

But Pascual-Leone didn't stop there. He had another group of volunteers do nothing but think about practicing the piano exercise. They played the simple piece in their heads, imagining how they would move their fingers to generate the notes. The study showed that the region of the motor cortex that controls the piano-playing fingers *expanded in the brains of volunteers who merely imagined playing the piece* just as it did in the brains of those who actually played it. He discovered that the mental rehearsal alone activated the same motor circuits as actual rehearsals, and generated the same result: the increased activation expanded that section of the motor cortex.

The power of your thoughts to expand your ability to lead and achieve is not just some metaphysical platitude—it's a physical, scientific, objective reality. Your thoughts literally change the structure and connections in your brain, which can make you biologically a better decision maker and leader.

See Through the Deception of Belief and Gain True Knowledge

When we start self-reflecting and understanding our thoughts and emotions, we discover that our beliefs are not necessarily truth. We start seeing where we've deceived ourselves in the past. We see where false beliefs have been hindering us by leading to poor decisions.

We see the world not as it is but as we are. And we are what we believe. If our beliefs are false and disempowering, they will lead to poor results. To the extent that our beliefs are false, we lack power to achieve our goals and create our ideal life. By managing our thoughts and emotions consistently, we start to become more honest with ourselves. We see our motivations and fears more clearly, which gives us the capacity to deal with them. We begin to see the deceptions in our beliefs, which are limiting us, and begin to access real knowledge of things as they really are.

"There is nothing either good or bad,
but thinking makes it so."

—WILLIAM SHAKESPEARE

One of my clients, Bill, owned a small business with his brother. They took over this family business from their father, who had built it from scratch. Both Bill and his brother had worked in the business their whole lives. Their father was much older and no longer able to provide the leadership of day-to-day operations.

Bill approached me to help him with the constant disagreements he and his brother were having regarding business decisions. They fought over who was ultimately in charge; how they should spend their time, money, and resources; and what their priorities should be to ensure the future success of the business.

After I spent time with Bill and his wife (who was also involved in the business), I concluded that the primary issue revolved around a deep-seated belief that Bill had about himself. This belief centered on issues of abandonment. The reason he was having so much trouble with his brother really stemmed from Bill's own conflict between his desire to no longer work in the business and the fear of becoming disconnected from the family. It wasn't until Bill could see this clearly that he was able to admit this to his family and eventually disengage from the business, leaving his brother to run it.

This took some time to accomplish, because Bill's fears of abandonment were extremely strong, and the emotions and illogical thoughts they created were very difficult for him to work through. It was exceedingly difficult for him to acknowledge that he was not interested in the business and to consider the issue of what he might do if he left the business. Bill's red coat moment had its start in his asking himself questions like, "How do I like to spend my time?" and "If I wasn't afraid of what my family thought, would I still choose to work in the family business?"

As Bill began to practice visualizing his perfect day—now without the negative emotion of what his family thought—it became apparent that he really enjoyed helping people, being with people, and being outdoors. As he began to see clearly how he wanted to spend his time, the next step was to look at occupations that would match these daily requirements. It turns out that Bill was a golfer in college and what he really wanted to do was be a golf instructor. Once he felt the emotional freedom to follow his passion, his life took on new meaning and his relationship with his brother and family improved dramatically. And, the business is doing just fine.

Buddha counseled, "All that we are is the result of what we have thought." Thoughts are at the center of every move, word, and choice.

"If you are pained by external things, it is not that they disturb you, but your own judgment of them. And it is in your power to wipe out that judgment now."
—MARCUS AURELIUS

Learning to change your negative thoughts can be difficult, so begin with a simple exercise. For the next thirty days, make the following changes in your life:

Choose one area of your life with which you are not happy. It can be a belief or behavior that you hold but would like to change.

It will be more difficult than you think, especially in the first ten days, so start simple. For instance, let's say your area of unhappiness involves a constant feeling of resentment toward a sibling, friend, or coworker. You have made all of your excuses for why you harbor this resentment. You have built a case for it in your head. Breaking down and discrediting your own "case" will be the primary challenge during your first thirty days.

Each day, recognize the negative belief or behavior when it occurs, and turn your mind against it in a conscious effort to act differently.

You know that feeling you get in the back of your throat or the pit of your stomach when this person (the sibling, friend, or coworker) does something that just drives you crazy? Recognize this negative feeling for what it really is—a negative thought interfering with your own life—and learn to turn the feeling into a positive. Think of something nice that the person has done for you. Learn to experience a sense of thankfulness in place of that resentment.

Affirm your new action in your heart as your new belief.

By the end of the thirty days, if you've made an

honest effort to maintain this exercise, you will discover warm thoughts about this person (the sibling, friend, or coworker). More important, you will have released yourself from resentment, so you can move forward without its weight dragging you down.

Replicate this exercise with other thoughts and beliefs that negatively affect your outlook. Whatever they are, no matter how big or small, internalizing a positive antithesis to that negative for only thirty days will help create a lifelong habit that can lead toward a profound sense of release and peace as you lose the unkind and unpleasant thoughts at long last.

As the Buddha says, "When the mind is pure, joy follows like a shadow that never leaves."

Accessing the Power of Autosuggestion

Autosuggestion is one of the most powerful things we can do to harness the power of our mind. The best way I know how to do this is to develop "mantras," or empowering and inspiring phrases, that reflect who we want to become, and which we repeat in our minds to drive them deep into our subconscious mind.

For example, you could repeat any of the following phrases throughout your meditation and your workdays:

- **"I can choose my own thoughts and actions."** Your thoughts and actions are your own, and therefore they are your choices to make. Stop making excuses for the negative thoughts you have and the hurtful actions you take. Instead, own your thoughts and actions and, in doing so, learn to be proud of them.
- **"Good thoughts and actions will produce good results."** As you embrace the knowledge that you are responsible for your thoughts, you will recognize the importance of thinking positively. Each time you think a positive thought in place of a negative one, you will begin to feel more exalted and confident in your abilities.
- **"My choices matter."** Our choices guide us toward love or hurt, contentment or depression. If you don't embrace the fact that your choices are determined by your thoughts and that your negative thoughts will produce negative choices, you will be perpetually trapped in a negative situation. Instead, realize that every choice has a

repercussion. If you make positive choices, you will never want to avoid their consequences.

- **"Believing this in my heart will make the difference."** The key is, and always will be, to accept these things in your heart. If you only take a surface-level approach, you will not be able to truly progress.

Moving from *Doing* to *Being*

Moving forward, the real difference maker in your life won't be *what you do*. It will be *who you become*. What we do flows from how we see the world, which flows from who we really are.

Personal reflection helps us to see ourselves more clearly and understand who we really are. With this knowledge, we can see where false beliefs are holding us back. Then, using the power of mantras, we can reverse our senses by changing our beliefs to make them more aligned with reality, and therefore more empowering. By doing this, you are actually conditioning your subconscious to respond differently in the future.

> *"There is something in every one of you that waits and listens for the sound of the genuine in yourself. It is the only true guide you will ever have. And if you cannot hear it, you will all of your life spend your days on the ends of strings that somebody else pulls."*
>
> —HOWARD THURMAN

In short, focusing on our thoughts and emotions changes who we are. And that internal change leads to smarter doing and better results in our external world. Going inside ourselves helps us to develop better thought processes. It helps us to access our intuition to make better decisions. It makes us more peaceful and happy, which then strengthens our relationships. We simply feel better all around, and that spreads to other people as well. People enjoy spending time with us and we create more value for them.

Consistency Is the Key

As with anything worthwhile, you won't see results

with these mental disciplines for the first few weeks of implementing them. It takes consistency over time to get the hang of it, to start getting real value from your meditation sessions, to start seeing results in your life. As motivational speaker and personal change expert Tony Robbins says: "If we want to direct our lives, we must take control of our consistent actions. It's not what we do once in a while that shapes our lives, but what we do consistently."

Three things are absolutely imperative to make meaningful internal adjustments in your life: knowledge, application, and practice. First, you must be able to see your situation clearly and understand the principles of thought and emotion that are constantly affecting you. Second, you must apply this knowledge on a regular basis by being aware of your thoughts and emotions. And third, you must practice some form of quiet personal reflection to allow yourself to calm yourself internally. In short you must "see the red coat" and reverse your senses on a regular basis. Most of my clients are able to achieve this.

Don, however, is a good example of an individual who tried but was unable to sustain his progress over time. In his case, there were times when he was able to see his situation pretty clearly and understood that his emotions would overwhelm him and affect his thoughts. But he was unwilling or unable to apply these principles on a regular basis to create internal change.

It's not that he didn't try. I believe his deep-seated beliefs about himself and the destructive emotions he experienced were so overwhelming that he simply did not have the ability to practice reversing his own senses on a regular basis. He was therefore unable to make any meaningful headway toward developing greater internal capacity.

Like Don, you may not necessarily like what you're currently experiencing, but the fear of the unknown is much greater and therefore keeps you where you are, repeating the same mistakes in life and feeling the same about yourself. Consistent practice is the key to breaking out of this inhibiting cycle. The Core Process is hard work and, like Don, there may be times when you get off track. Don't be discouraged when this happens—just stay committed to rising every time you fall.

This also underscores the importance of using a life coach or mentor to hold you accountable to the process and to motivate and encourage you throughout. In some cases, therapy may even be appropriate to help you deal with your strongest emotional undertows. This does not have to be—and in fact should not be—a do-it-yourself process, at least in the initial stages. Once you learn the process, it becomes easier to identify and deal with destructive and limiting thoughts and emotions through meditation, mantras, and exercises.

In any case, consistency is the key. As personal development guru Jim Rohn says, "Success is neither magical nor mysterious. Success is the natural consequence of consistently applying basic fundamentals." Leadership expert John Maxwell builds on that foundation when he writes, "Small disciplines repeated with consistency every day lead to great achievements gained slowly over time." The mental disciplines I've described in this book are basic fundamentals of success. Applied consistently, they will transform your life over time.

Case Study: Benjamin Franklin

Printer, writer, inventor, diplomat, businessman, musician, scientist, humorist, civic leader, international celebrity, Founding Father, legend, and polymath: Benjamin Franklin is certainly one of the most extraordinary people who have ever lived. He accomplished more in his lifetime than few people even dream of. Among other things, he invented the lightning rod, bifocals, the Franklin stove, a carriage odometer, and the "glass armonica." He was instrumental in building a fire department and a university, among many other civic organizations.

Franklin's accomplishments were not the product of wealth or privilege. He was born into a poor family and only received two years of formal schooling. He started out as a printer, and through hard work and ingenuity became wealthy and then moved on to other pursuits.

But beyond hard work, Franklin would attribute his success to his drive to constantly improve himself. At the age of twenty, after engaging in some youthful follies, he set the lofty goal of attaining moral perfection. As he wrote in his autobiography, "I conceiv'd the bold and arduous project of arriving at moral perfection. I wish'd to live without committing any fault at any time; I would conquer all that either natural inclination, custom, or company might lead me into." In other words, he resolved to manage his thoughts and emotions ("natural inclination") wisely.

Understanding the power of autosuggestion to aid

him in accomplishing his goal, Franklin developed and wrote down the following thirteen virtues:

1. TEMPERANCE. Eat not to dullness; drink not to elevation.

2. SILENCE. Speak not but what may benefit others or yourself; avoid trifling conversation.

3. ORDER. Let all your things have their places; let each part of your business have its time.

4. RESOLUTION. Resolve to perform what you ought; perform without fail what you resolve.

5. FRUGALITY. Make no expense but to do good to others or yourself; i.e., waste nothing.

6. INDUSTRY. Lose no time; be always employ'd in something useful; cut off all unnecessary actions.

7. SINCERITY. Use no hurtful deceit; think innocently and justly, and, if you speak, speak accordingly.

8. JUSTICE. Wrong none by doing injuries, or omitting the benefits that are your duty.

9. MODERATION. Avoid extremes; forbear resenting injuries so much as you think they deserve.

10. CLEANLINESS. Tolerate no uncleanliness in body, cloaths, or habitation.
11. TRANQUILLITY. Be not disturbed at trifles, or at accidents common or unavoidable.
12. CHASTITY. Rarely use venery but for health or offspring, never to dullness, weakness, or the injury of your own or another's peace or reputation.
13. HUMILITY. Imitate Jesus and Socrates.

To track his adherence to these virtues, Franklin carried around a small book of charts, consisting of a column for each day of the week and thirteen rows marked with the first letter of his thirteen virtues.

Franklin evaluated himself at the end of each day, placing a dot next to each virtue he had violated. His goal was to minimize his marks, which would indicate a virtuous life free of vice. Each week Franklin would focus on one virtue in particular. He would place the virtue at the top of his weekly chart and include a "short precept" explaining its meaning. After thirteen weeks he would move through all thirteen virtues and would then start the process again.

Initially, to his dismay, his chart was full of marks. But as he stuck with his program consistently, the marks began to diminish. He reported that, "Tho' I never arrived at the perfection I had been so ambitious of obtaining, but fell far short of it, yet I was, by the endeavour, a better and a happier man than I otherwise should have been if I had not attempted it."

By managing his thoughts and emotions, Franklin increased his internal capacity to lead and achieve. He said, "Being ignorant is not so much a shame as being unwilling to learn." He added that "An investment in knowledge always pays the best interest." And I'm certain he would agree that no knowledge is more important than self-knowledge.

CHAPTER 7

OVERVIEW OF THE CORE PROCESS

NOW THAT YOU ARE ACQUAINTED WITH THE DETAILS of the five principles of the Core Process, the actual process itself will make more sense to you. The Core Process I've designed is a systematic method that assists individuals in developing their internal capacity, which is your ability to think and see clearly, maintain positive and optimistic thoughts, make wise decisions, and feel calm, peaceful, and confident regardless of what is happening in your external world. The Core Process is designed to accomplish the following objectives:

- Educate the participant.
- Create clarity and understanding regarding basic universal principles that apply to all.
- Uncover specific core beliefs of the individual.

Once these objectives have been attained at some level, the next step is to apply the self-knowledge you've gained to experience the benefit of these principles. Finally, there are multiple exercises to practice in conjunction with applying these principles that will produce consistent calm and clarity of thought.

In a nutshell, the Core Process is a program for developing internal capacity rooted in the process of knowledge, application, and practice. The following is a detailed description of each step in the program, what is involved, and what you should experience as a result of working through the Core Process.

In my experience of taking clients through the process, a successful transformation requires a minimum of sixty days. The first phase is all about uncovering your core beliefs—especially subconscious ones—that may be limiting your productivity and progress. Once these have been revealed, it takes time to reprogram your mind to accept and live new, more empowering beliefs.

STEP 1: GAINING SELF-KNOWLEDGE, 30 HOURS OF FOCUSED WORK

Understanding the five core principles is critical to

making any meaningful headway toward developing your internal capacity. As you begin to see and embrace these concepts about the influence thoughts and emotions have over one another and their relevance to creating sustainable success, you will be motivated to apply them on a regular basis.

The simple notion of cause and effect (everything internal is cause and everything external is effect) will take you a long way toward focusing your effort in a productive direction. That direction will be toward discovering the subconscious messaging you received as a child that affects you in your adult life.

This specific work involves taking a walk down memory lane. (I'll get to the specific questions you'll need to ask yourself in a moment.) This usually takes about ten to fifteen hours and should be done with another person. For best results, I recommend a professional coach or therapist. Please note that reflecting on the past may evoke strong emotions, such as anger or depression. If this happens to you, it may be wise to seek professional counseling to help you deal with the emotions in a positive way.

The more you are able to reflect on your life without judgment, the easier it will be to see the recurring behaviors that are produced by the internal messaging you have programmed internally to protect yourself.

Start at the beginning of your life. Even though you have no memories of that time, you do know something about the environment in which you were raised, and who your parents, siblings, and extended family members were. This is the environment that produces the earliest instincts of survival and what is required for a person to feel loved, safe, and secure. Continue on through your life recalling your earliest memories. Focus on and try to visualize where you were, who you were with, and how you felt about what was happening in that moment.

For most people, it is not necessary to do deep and intensive therapy. The goal is simply to understand in an honest and meaningful way the influences that shaped your initial paradigms.

"Freedom is useless if we don't exercise it as characters making choice . . . We are free to change the stories by which we live. Because we are genuine characters, and not mere puppets, we can choose our defining stories. We can do so because we actively participate in the creation of our stories. We are co-authors as well as characters. Few things are so encouraging as the realization that things can be different and that we have a role in making them so."

—DANIEL TAYLOR

Take this exercise all the way up to your current life. I have found it helpful to break life segments into five-year chunks. For example, ages zero to five, ages six to ten, ages eleven to eighteen, and so forth up to your present age. However you decide to break it up, do so in a way that produces the most vivid memories. I would also suggest not spending more than two hours in any one sitting.

Use the following pages to write down your memories, insights, and internal programming. Your internal

programming is your neuro responses to external stimuli. As cognitive neuroscientists say, neurons that fire
together wire together. For example, suppose your
mother yelled at you when you were eight years old
for talking too much when guests were over, and that
deeply affected you. Write down the lesson and message
you internalized from that experience (e.g. ,"When I
talk too much I am an embarrassment."), and do that
for any other experience you can remember that programmed your thoughts about yourself and the world
around you.

At the end of this process you should be able to
identify at some level your own specific messaging that
sits at your core.

Memories That Have Caused My Internal Programming

Use the following pages to write down experiences you remember from your life that have contributed to your internal programming. For example, "I remember my English teacher telling me I would never amount to much when I flunked her final research paper. Much of my drive to achieve has been to prove her wrong."

MEMORY

_____

_____

_____

_____

_____

_____

_____

_____

INFLUENCE ON MY INTERNAL PROGRAMMING

_____

_____

_____

_____

_____

_____

_____

_____

_____

_____

_____

_____

_____

_____

In most cases, an individual's red coat moment is produced during this process as he or she begins to see the correlation between the five principles and their own thoughts, emotions, and behavior over the course of their life.

STEP 2: APPLICATION, ONGOING DURING THE 60-DAY PROGRAM

Applying the knowledge you are gaining during this process is essential to producing tangible results. Remember, knowledge without application is mere information that will produce nothing. For the athlete who understands the physiological results of a specific exercise but then never exercises, there will be no physical benefit! The same applies to this process in your life.

The method for applying your knowledge in this case is by developing self-awareness. Becoming aware of your thoughts and emotions, combined with the understanding of the five principles, will produce dramatic results. In most cases, this will require you to reverse your senses as you are applying these techniques.

Thought Awareness

This may seem simple, but how many people have actually examined their thoughts on a regular basis? I am talking about your running stream of consciousness—what you're thinking when you walk into Starbucks and the line is out the door and you are running late, or when you are stuck in traffic, or when . . . You get the drift. Remember, what you think, how you think matters—not just some of the time but *all of the time.*

When I actually started to monitor my thoughts through internal observation, I was shocked at how negative and critical most of my stream-of-consciousness thinking was. Some people like to keep journals of their observations for future reference or so they can visually see their progress. Once you begin to form this habit, the ongoing purpose is to recognize these thoughts and change them. For me, the most effective means is to begin to recite a positive mantra to counter the negative or critical thought. My favorite mantra is: "I am whole, strong, clear, and powerful. I am loving, harmonious, and happy." Engaging in repeating a mantra should result in dissipating the negative thoughts. I have found that over time I have fewer negative thoughts and I am less critical of others.

Emotional Awareness

Being aware of how you are feeling does not come naturally for most people. In order to become more aware, begin to identify things in your external world that trigger an emotional response in/from you. Pay attention to how you are feeling and ask yourself the question, "What am I feeling, and why?" This may seem simple and straightforward, but it does require effort to form the habit.

My Emotional Triggers

As you become aware of your emotional triggers, write them down here (using the format of the suggested examples):

THE EMOTIONAL SOURCE OF THE TRIGGER	WHAT CAUSED THE TRIGGER?
I was deeply upset when my customer wouldn't take my phone call.	I remembered how my dad wouldn't let me call him at work, and how emotionally disengaged he was from me.
I felt anxious when my partners and I discussed moving our business to another city.	I've always disliked moving ever since my family moved when I was thirteen years old and I lost all my friends and had to readjust to a new city.

As you become more aware of your feelings, you will begin to see how dramatically they influence your thoughts. For example, on his way out the door to his office, Mike spills coffee on his tie, triggering anger. He starts thinking about the time lost and the stress of all his deadlines, and it puts him in a foul mood for the rest of the morning. At the breakfast table, Jan gets into an argument with her daughter about what she's wearing. She starts worrying about her daughter's choices, and she feels distraught all day.

At times, our emotions are much stronger than our external situations should dictate because of our subconscious emotional wounds. This is why the emotional triggers exercise above is so valuable; it helps you to uncover those wounds so you can deal with the emotions more appropriately. The best way to manage emotion is to first be aware of the emotion, then to observe your thoughts during the experience. Awareness is the cornerstone to being able to create just enough distance between the emotion and the reflexive behavior driven by the emotion. In so doing, you are better able to establish more constructive thoughts and behaviors in the moment and become less reactive in the future. Consistent autosuggestion is an invaluable tool to this process, as it is how you reprogram your mind.

"You are in charge of how you react to the people and events in your life. You can either give negativity power over your life or you can choose happiness instead. Take control and choose to focus on what is important in your life. Those who cannot live fully often become destroyers of life."

—ANAÏS NIN

Autosuggestion

Autosuggestion is simply the process of reciting some form of mantra or statement full of positive and optimistic references. When you observe some form of negative thought process developing in your mind, immediately replace it with your positive, affirmative mantra.

You can also routinely recite your mantra in your mind on a regular basis to produce more positive subconscious experiences in the future. Remember, your conscious mind is your ability to reason and choose in the present, and your subconscious mind is your instinctive, emotional desires rooted in past experiences. You can shape your subconscious future through the thoughts you entertain today.

While this may seem simple, it is difficult to practice initially, but if you develop the habit your future experiences will be amazingly different.

The best way to get started is to make a daily commitment to observing your thoughts and emotions. Begin the day with a simple suggestion to yourself: "Today I will do my best to observe my thoughts and emotions and practice my positive mantra: 'I am in charge of my thoughts regardless of what I am feeling.'" This practice has had a profound impact on both my clients and me. We've learned to become more peaceful and less reactive to negative external stimuli.

Visualization

Visualization is a process where you are actually seeing in your mind's eye a picture of what you would like to see actualized in real life. Creating these images in your mind will move you toward realizing them in your external world.

"Dream lofty dreams, and as you dream, so shall you become. Your Vision is the promise of what you shall one day be. Your Ideal is the prophecy of what you shall at last unveil."

—JAMES ALLEN

For some this may be easy, but for most it is very difficult to hold a steady picture in your mind for any period of time. Consistent practice is required to develop this skill.

Simply sit quietly, breathe deeply, relax your body, and picture some scene in your mind that is pleasing to you or that you idealize. The image may not be clear at first, but through diligent practice the image should begin to take shape. As this image becomes very focused, you will be well on your way to manifesting it in your external world.

Try and be patient, for what you are visualizing will take time to develop. As with everything, there is a specific law of growth that all thoughts will follow as they work their way from the internal to the external. Remember, there are no miracles, so if you are expecting one you may be disappointed and miss out on the actual progression of this very powerful source to produce what you want out of life.

STEP 3: PRACTICE, DAILY DURING 60-DAY PROGRAM

In the Core Process program, the term *practice* refers to some type of meditation or quiet personal reflection. The purpose is to intentionally take the time to quiet your thoughts and your body, to demonstrate to yourself that you have the power to do so.

In the beginning you may be restless and fidgety, but after the first week you should find that it is not too much trouble to carve out fifteen minutes of your day for this purpose.

If you have never attempted this in the past or have not succeeded in establishing a meaningful practice, I would suggest the following routine:

- Find a place in your home that is comfortable and private. Go to the same place each time you practice.
- For the first two weeks, just sit quietly, take in

three very deep breaths, and exhale slowly. Then simply allow yourself to sit for five or ten minutes—whatever you can tolerate comfortably—and observe your thoughts. Finish by taking one last deep breath and exhaling slowly. That's it!

- For the next two weeks, do the same thing, only this time during the five- to ten-minute period, focus on your breathing. See yourself breathing in and out. If your mind starts to wander, just observe this and refocus your attention on your breath.

- During week five you should be able to sit quietly and now engage in intentional thought. Visualize in your mind thoughts that are important to you, something that brings you joy, peace, and harmony, and perhaps some objective you would like to accomplish.

By this time you should be able to quiet your mind very effectively. Once you are able to do this, a whole new world of possibilities will begin to open up.

If you miss a day, no worries, just continue wherever you left off.

Your quiet mind practice will begin to take on a life of its own once you get through the initial discomfort, and where you take it truly depends on how much time you devote to the practice of meditation and where you take your thoughts. As a result of this practice, you should experience a calmer, clearer, and less emotional reaction to your external world. As a result, you will see corresponding improvements in your decision-making and intrapersonal skills.

* * *

If you commit yourself to the Core Process program for sixty days, I can absolutely guarantee the following benefits:

- More internal peace
- Less anxiety
- More clarity of thought
- Better overall health
- The ability to hold and maintain positive optimistic thoughts
- A noticeable positive change in your external world

I highly recommend that you devote the full sixty days to this process to achieve the best results. Even spending as little as ten or fifteen minutes a day on these disciplines will give you benefits of the Core Process. It will just take longer to receive that benefit.

The most important thing is that you put yourself on the right path, that you fish in the right pond. As you do so, your ability to reverse your senses will be strengthened, and your internal capacity to lead and achieve will be greatly enhanced.

BREAK THROUGH YOUR CEILINGS BY FOCUSING ON THE RIGHT THINGS

*"The ideal held steadily in mind attracts the
necessary conditions for its fulfillment."*
—*Charles F. Haanel*

WHAT IF YOU COULD BREAK FREE FROM EVERYTHING that's held you back in the past? What if you could discover the answers to your most pressing questions, the solutions to your most distressing problems? What if you could eliminate your feelings of stress, worry, fear, and inadequacy and reverse your senses to replace them with feelings of peace, joy, and contentment? What if you could stop and appreciate your successes and achievements, and feel satisfied with them?

You absolutely can, and you already have the ability to do so. The answers, solutions, and feelings you seek are within you. Your thoughts hold the key to break you out of your box of limitations.

By reading this book, you've realized that in order to become a better leader and achieve more you must develop your internal capacity. You've realized the importance of managing your thoughts and emotions, of channeling them toward productivity. Your external results are the product of your internal capacity. Your physical capabilities can never exceed your mental strength and awareness.

What you focus on grows. If you're like me, you've been focusing a lot on your problems and feelings of discomfort. And as you do so, they continue to grow. We're funny creatures: We don't want to feel dissatisfaction, so we focus on our feelings of dissatisfaction and their cause. As a result, those feelings grow.

"We are personally responsible for most of the major events in our lives and for all our responses to these events. Recognition of this fact opens up a vision of human reality that is at once vivid and durable."

—ROBERT GRUDIN

The only way to break through our ceilings of complexity is to focus on the answers and solutions. The only way to get out of tough and uncomfortable situations is to first create a vision of an ideal, then stop focusing on the negative situation and instead focus on the ideal. As Charles F. Haanel wrote,

> We can form our own mental images through our own interior process of thought regardless of the thoughts of others, regardless of exterior conditions, regardless of environment of every kind, and it is by the exercise of this power that we can control our own destiny, body, mind, and soul. It is by the exercise of this power that we can take our fate out of the hands of chance, and consciously make for ourselves the experiences which we desire, because when we consciously realize a condition that condition will eventually manifest in our lives . . .

He also counseled, "If you wish to eliminate fear, then concentrate on courage. If you wish to eliminate lack, then concentrate on abundance. If you wish to eliminate disease, then concentrate on health. Always concentrate on the ideal as an already existing fact. This is the Elohim, the germ cell, the life principle which goes forth and enters in and becomes, sets in motion those causes which guide, direct, and bring about the

necessary relation, which eventually manifest in form."
In order to do this, you must reverse the senses.

This is why mindful meditation has been such a
powerful force in my life, and why I hope you'll consider it as a tool in your life as well. Without taking
time to focus on our ideal, we get caught up in the
demands of daily living. It's easy to get caught up "in
the thick of thin things," as Stephen R. Covey puts it.
Or, to use Covey's terms again, we waste our time and
energy on things that are urgent but not important.

Taking quiet time to reflect helps us to focus on
the things that are truly important in our lives. It
helps us slice through the clutter of negative thoughts
and emotions and all the things competing for our
time and attention, in order to see things more clearly.
Like Oskar Schindler, it helps us to see past all the
junk in the world and to see the red coat—to see what
matters most, to see which path to take, to see the
right decision.

Thus far in your journey you've been asking the
question "What should I do?" Now you know that
the more useful question is "How should I think and
be?" For, as self-help author Frances Larimer Warner
said, "We have discovered that premeditated, orderly

thinking for a purpose matures that purpose into fixed form, so that we may be absolutely sure of the result of our dynamic experiment."

But as New Thought Movement author Orison Swett Marden wrote in his book *Pushing to the Front*, "The possibilities of thought training are infinite, its consequence eternal, and yet few take the pains to direct their thinking into channels that will do them good, but instead leave all to chance." I hope you don't leave your thoughts to chance while expecting your actions to carry the day. Your bold actions have taken you thus far in your journey. Now it's time to rely on the power of your thoughts and the reversing of your senses to achieve internal harmony and thus produce greater external results. As you do so, you will break through your ceilings and take your life to a whole new level.

ACKNOWLEDGMENTS

There are so many people who have had an influence on this book that it is impossible to acknowledge them all. However, I'd like to publicly thank the people who have had the most impact on this collaborative work.

First, I would like to thank my Young President's Organization and World President's Organization Forum mates who assisted me in my transition from CEO to advisor and consultant. Without their support and encouragement this never would have been possible.

I would also like to thank my many clients who have been willing to trust in this process and allowed me to be a part of that experience. Your insights and experiences have shaped the very fabric of this book.

I am not a writer, so in order to fully get the message across it was imperative to find a skilled and gifted writer to do so. I cannot thank Stephen Palmer enough for his uncompromising professionalism and dedication in actually putting the core process into words. Stephen, you are a true talent!

A special thanks to my father who has always been

a true support to me and was willing to engage in and benefit from the core process for himself early on. This was a key milestone in convincing me that the core process was worth developing and refining for others.

Thanks to my incredible children who inspire me constantly with their wisdom and unconditional love for their dad. Noelle and Mack, I love you very much!

And finally, to my beautiful and loving wife, Lisa, thank you from the bottom of my heart for your patience and understanding during the creation of this work and always. You are and will always be the rock that God has put in my life to soften my edges.

BIBLIOGRAPHY

Allen, James. *As a Man Thinketh.* Nashville. 1934.

Ariely, Dan. *Predictably Irrational: The Hidden Forces That Shape Our Decisions.* New York: HarperCollins, 2008.

"Back to the Future at Apple." Businessweek.com. May 24, 1998. http://www.businessweek.com/stories/1998-05-24/back-to -the-future-at-apple.

Begley, Sharon. *Train Your Mind, Change Your Brain: How a New Science Reveals Our Extraordinary Potential to Transform Ourselves.* New York: Ballantine Books, 2008.

Branson, Richard. *Like a Virgin: Secrets They Won't Teach You at Business School.* New York: Penguin, 2012.

Branson, Richard. "Richard Branson: Five Secrets to Business Success." Entrepreneur.com. September 9, 2010. http://www.entrepreneur.com/article/217284#.

Brogran, Chris. "The Bad Boy of Business Wants You to Be Good." Success.com. Accessed December 11, 2013. http://www.success.com/article/the-bad-boy-of-business -wants-you-to-be-good.

Burns, David D. *Feeling Good: The New Mood Therapy.* New York: Avon Books, 1980.

Covey, Stephen R. *The 7 Habits of Highly Effective People.* New York: Free Press, 1989.

Deaton, Dennis. *Ownership Spirit: The One Grand Key That Changes Everything Else.* Mesa, AZ: Quma Learning Systems, Inc., 2009.

Duhigg, Charles. *The Power of Habit: Why We Do What We Do in Life and Business.* New York: Random House, 2012.

Eagleman, David. *Incognito: The Secret Lives of the Brain.* New York: Pantheon, 2011.

Emmons, Robert and Michael McCullough. "Counting Blessings Versus Burdens: An Experimental Investigation of Gratitude and Subjective Well-Being in Daily Life." *Journal of Personality and Social Psychology* 84, no. 2 (2003): 377–389. doi: 10.1037/0022-3514.84.2.377.

Franklin, Benjamin. *The Autobiography of Benjamin Franklin.* Philadelphia: J.P. Lippincott & Co., 1868.

Goleman, Daniel. *Emotional Intelligence: Why It Can Matter More Than IQ.* New York: Scientific American, 1994.

Goleman, Daniel. "What Makes a Leader." *Harvard Business Review* (Jan. 2004). http://hbr.org/2004/01/what-makes-a-leader.

Grudin, Robert. *The Grace of Great Things: Creativity and Innovation.* New York: Houghton Mifflin, 1990.

Haanel, Charles F. *The Master Key System.* St. Louis, MO: Psychology Publishing, 1916.

Hill, Napoleon. *Think and Grow Rich.* 1937.

Isaacson, Walter. *Steve Jobs.* New York: Simon & Schuster, 2011.

Joseph, R. *The Right Brain and the Unconscious: Discovering the Stranger Within.* Cambridge, MA: Perseus, 1992.

Kushner, Harold. *Living a Life that Matters: Resolving the Conflict Between Conscience and Success.* New York: Anchor Books, 2002.

Lusseyran, Jacques. *And There Was Light: Autobiography of Jacques Lusseyran, 2nd ed.* Sandpoint, ID: Morning Light Press, 2006.

Lyubomirsky, Sonja. *The How of Happiness: A New Approach to Getting the Life You Want.* New York: Penguin, 2007.

Maltz, Maxwell. *Psycho-Cybernetics.* New York: Pocket Books, 1960.

Marden, Orison Swett. *Pushing to the Front.* 1894. Reprint. Radford, VA: Wilder Publications, 2007.

Packer, Boyd K. "Inspiring Music-Worthy Thoughts." *Ensign* (January 1974). http://www.lds.org/ensign/1974/01 /inspiring-music-worthy-thoughts.

Peale, Norman Vincent. *The Power of Positive Thinking.* New York: Fireside, 1956.

Poscente, Vince. *The Ant and the Elephant.* Dallas, TX: Be Invinceable Group, 2004.

Potter-Efron, Ronald. *Healing the Angry Brain: How Understanding the Way Your Brain Works Can Help You Control Anger and Aggression.* Oakland, CA: New Harbinger Publications, 2012.

Sampson, Anthony. *Mandela: The Authorized Biography.* New York: Vintage Books, 1999.

Scheier, Michael and Charles Carver. "Optimism, Coping, and Health: Assessment and Implications of Generalized Outcome Expectancies." *Health Psychology* 4, no. 3 (1985): 219–247. doi: 10.1037//0278-6133.4.3.219.

Seligman, Martin. *Authentic Happiness: Using the New Positive Psychology to Realize Your Potential for Lasting Fulfillment.* New York: The Free Press, 2002.

Seligman, Martin. *Learned Optimism: How to Change Your Mind and Your Life.* New York: Vintage, 2006.

Ten Boom, Corrie. *The Hiding Place.* Edited by Elizabeth and John Sherrill. Grand Rapids, MI: Chosen Books, 2006.

Villarica, Hans. "How the Power of Positive Thinking Won Scientific Credibility." The *Atlantic* magazine interview with Michael Scheier. April 23, 2012. http://www.theatlantic .com/health/archive/2012/04/how-the-power-of-positive -thinking-won-scientific-credibility/256223/.

Wagner, Ullrich, Steffen Gais, Hilde Haider, Rolf Verleger, and Jan Born. "Sleep Inspires Insight." *Nature* 427 (January 22, 2004): 352–355. doi: 10.1038/nature02223.

Wallace, David Foster. "This Is Water." Full text of commencement speech at Kenyon College in 2005. September 19, 2008. Intelligentlife.com. http://www.more intelligentlife.com/story/david-foster-wallace-in-his-own -words.

ABOUT THE AUTHOR

Martin Hubbard has an extensive and diverse background. After graduating from the University of Redlands with a bachelor's degree in economics in 1984, he went on to complete his master's degree in psychology from the California Graduate Institute in 1987.

During the first five years of his career, Martin worked with families and individuals in a hospital facility to help them reveal their core issues. Ultimately, he moved from the clinical side of the facility to the business side and participated in the venture capital start-up of a healthcare company that focused on implementing psychiatric treatment programs in hospitals nationwide. During his tenure, he oversaw the growth of this company from a single operating unit to a multi-location organization with a national presence.

In 1994, Martin made a career transition by leading a group of investors in the acquisition of Abbey Rents. As CEO, he was responsible for the turnaround of a distressed asset, and under his leadership, Abbey Rents returned to profitability, tripling in size and regaining its reputation in the industry as a high-quality provider of services.

In 2000, Martin positioned the company for acquisition, and by midyear it was sold to the industry consolidator generating twelve times the return on the investors' equity investment. Martin stayed on in a leadership role, assisting the buyer with their growth initiative and eventually participating in their exit strategy in 2006.

Martin's work and passion is to develop the tools and method of delivery that translate into meaningful and life-changing experiences for others. He is currently the principal of Core Advisors, an organization that specializes in assisting individuals with achieving success and significance in their personal and professional lives. He has combined his personal experience, educational background, and professional success as a business leader to develop the Core Process.™ This method is uniquely designed to systematically help others accomplish their goals in life.

Martin has been a member of the Young Presidents Organization International for the past twelve years and is currently a member of the World Presidents Organization. He is an active member of the Social

Enterprise Network within WPO and is committed to supporting the values and purpose of corporate social responsibility within the world community.

CPSIA information can be obtained
at www.ICGtesting.com
Printed in the USA
FSOW03n1450201016
26378FS